Wedding
PLANS

for living life well!

50
UNIQUE THEMES
FOR THE
WEDDING OF
YOUR DREAMS

SHARON DLUGOSCH

BRIGHTON PUBLICATIONS, INC.
PRINTED IN THE UNITED STATES OF AMERICA

Brighton Publications, Inc.

Copyright © 1989, revised 1996 by Sharon E. Dlugosch

Brighton Publications, Inc.
P.O. Box 120706
St. Paul, MN 55112-0706
612-636-2220

First Edition: 1989
Second Edition: 1996

Library of Congress Cataloging-in-Publication Data
Dlugosch, Sharon.
    Wedding plans : 50 unique themes for the wedding of your
dreams / Sharon Dlugosch.
        p.   cm.
    Includes indexes.
    1. Marriage customs and rites—United States—Handbooks,
manuals, etc. 2. Marriage customs and rites—United States—
Handbooks, manuals, etc.   I. Title.
GT2703.D48   1996
392'.5—dc20   96-12326
                                                                   CIP

ISBN 0-918420-28-8

Printed in the United States of America

Acknowledgement

A round of applause to everyone who gave advice and enthusiastic suggestions. I especially want to thank Virginia Sande, who played an important role in the development of this book. As floral consultant, she created many of the bouquets and centerpiece ideas featured in this book. Everyone should have the opportunity to work with such refreshing talent.

Contents

INTRODUCTION   7

1   WEDDING PLAN QUESTIONS   9

2   DECORATIVE THEMES   18

3   STYLE SETTING THEMES   27

4   REGIONAL THEMES   35

5   TIMELESS THEMES   42

6   HOLIDAY THEMES   50

7   HERITAGE THEMES   58

8   DESTINATION THEMES   64

9   SEASONAL THEMES   72

10   SPECIAL SITE THEMES   78

11   TODAY'S CEREMONY THEMES   86

12   WEDDING PLAN LIST   96

13   ATTENDANT GIFT GUIDE   99

14   INVITATION GUIDE   101

15   CENTERPIECE GUIDE   103

16 TABLE SETTING GUIDE   108

17 FAVOR GUIDE   113

18 WEDDING CAKE GUIDE   117

19 DECORATIVE RECIPE GUIDE   119

20 DECORATIONS FOR THE RECEPTION GUIDE   122

21 DECORATIONS FOR THE CEREMONY GUIDE   127

22 MUSIC GUIDE   129

23 FLORAL BOUQUET GUIDE   131

24 FASHION GUIDE   135

25 MEMORY MAKER GUIDE   138

26 YOUNGER SET GUIDE   140

27 RICE-THROWING GUIDE   142

28 ACTIVITY AND ATTRACTIONS GUIDE   143

29 WEDDING TOASTS   145

    WEDDING PLAN PAGES   147

    THEME INDEX   153

    GENERAL INDEX   155

Introduction

When we think of weddings, we think of fun, excitement, pretty dresses, beautiful flowers, and a wonderful time. Weddings are a most memorable event, something everyone eagerly anticipates.

Now it's your turn to plan a wedding. First you experience euphoria, and then sooner or later nervousness, procrastination, blankness, bewilderment, or even panic may enter the picture. This is the time to collect your thoughts and take command of the situation. In other words, focus on the kind of wedding you will most enjoy.

To help give direction to your wedding plans, choose a theme for your wedding. Like most people, you want your wedding to be as meaningful and beautiful as it can be—a wedding to create lasting memories for everyone involved. Choosing a theme can help you create this kind of wedding.

The aim of this book is to provide a variety of themes to fit any personality, situation, or time of year. Your theme can be whimsical, traditional, glamorous or low key, sentimental or upbeat. Select the theme that appeals to you and you'll enjoy not only the wedding day itself, but the planning and energy invested beforehand.

Once you've decided on your theme, coordinate it by selecting flower arrangements, table settings, colors, dress, and decorations that enhance it rather than detract from it. Work with the materials and resources you have on hand, and learn to be flexible.

As you work your way through myriad details of planning a wedding, you'll want to use the Wedding Party List. I've included the list to help you keep organized and feel you're in control.

I've also included a list of helpful wedding guides. The guides are there so you can, at a glance, find a solution to a particular wedding dilemma. Though you may be working with one theme, there's always a chance that an idea from another theme will be the perfect solution.

It's possible, too, you may decide to use only a few ideas from one theme. On the other hand, you may decide to mix and match ideas from several themes. Good for you! That means you're well on your way to making your wedding personally and uniquely yours.

Whatever you decision, I know you'll enjoy your wedding day as well as the preparations for your wedding. After all, the planning and decisions should be almost as much fun as the wedding day itself. Once you see the possibilities, I believe that will hold true for you.

1. Wedding Plan Questions

Planning a wedding can seem overwhelming and difficult at best. Reading these questions and answers should help you to focus and give you a sense of direction. At the least, it will start you thinking about wonderful and creative possibilities. So take a deep breath and enjoy the first step toward planning a meaningful and beautiful wedding.

Q: I'm searching for a connection, something that will tie all the elements of our wedding together. It goes without saying that we want to make the day memorable and special.

—Waiting for Inspiration

Dear Waiting:

Themes are just the thing to start your creative juices cooking. The inspiration for the theme that's best for you can come from several sources. Does your favorite room have country decor? Then you'll be excited about the I Love Country theme. Are your friends into fifties rock and roll? If so, everyone will enjoy going back in time to the Fabulous Fifties theme. Are you a one-of-a-kind with a distinctive style all your own? Be sure to look at the Casual Chic theme. As you can see, the possibilities are varied and endless. Read through all the themes to make sure you don't miss the one, inspired idea that will make your wedding memorable!

Q: I warned my parents well in advance that I wanted a traditional wedding with all the trimmings. Now that the time is here, we need all the help we can find to make everything perfect.

—Traditionally Minded

Dear Traditionally:

You're not alone. Today's trend is toward glamorous and traditional weddings. You'll find plenty of cherished wedding customs and rituals in the Traditionally Yours theme. To make sure you're aware of all the possibilities for your day of days, review the Banquet Room and Evening Formal themes. These themes will give you a good start at making your dreams come true.

Q: Everything is planned to perfection except for one thing . . . gifts for our attendants. We want them to have a memento of the day just to show how much they are appreciated.

—Grateful

Dear Grateful:

Wedding couples tell me that this one small detail of attendants' gifts can end up as one large headache. To help solve this problem, there is a long list of suggested gifts in the Attendant Gift Guide section. Just turn to the guide, and you'll be well on your way to solving this particular problem. In reading through the themes, you'll notice it's much easier to solve this problem if you have a specific theme for your wedding.

Q: Of course, getting married is serious stuff, but I would like to take a lighthearted approach to the celebrating afterwards. Nothing involved, just some pretty decorations and a pleasant atmosphere.

—Fancy Free

Dear Free:

You're just the candidate for the Decorative Themes offering. The Balloon Bash, Gifts from the Sea, and Fanfare all create the kind of gay and colorful spirit you're looking for in a celebration. If you have a swimming pool area available, by all means consider the Poolside theme. When it's atmosphere you want, you can't beat a poolside party.

Q: This wedding is very important to us. How can we personalize the ceremony and reception to make our day truly special?
—Searching

Dear Searching:

Look no further, because I have a set of themes that result in the kind of wedding only because you are who you are. Let me explain. Today, everyone is becoming more aware (and proud) of their heritage. What better time than the happy occasion of a wedding to share your heritage with your guests. Be sure to look over all the Heritage themes for several different ways to display the best of your heritage. On a more personal note, the Sentimental Reasons theme brings fond memories of family weddings past to your wedding today. Don't miss these personal ways to create family traditions at your wedding.

Q: This will be a second marriage for both of us. We're as excited about this wedding as if it were our first. Are there any taboos or limitations to observe for a second wedding?
—A New Beginning

Dear Beginning:

No taboos and certainly no limitations exist in the wedding world today. Your wedding is about new beginnings and hope for the future, the kind of sentiment the Second Marriage theme expresses. Be sure, though, to read through all the themes so you'll be certain to have the kind of wedding you want the second time around.

Q: My attendants will be carrying parasols color-matched to their gowns. It occurred to me that it might be fun to include parasols in the decorating scheme, as well.

—Shades of Scarlett

Dear Scarlett:

Not only the decorating but all aspects of the wedding can be enhanced with this romantic accessory. The Parasol Style theme shows how parasols can embellish your complete wedding from invitations to the wedding cake table as well as inspire the perfect attendants' gifts. So pop open the parasols and give them a twirl!

Q: Our wedding date is set, and it happens to be close to a major holiday. Is this going to create problems?

—Holiday Dilemma

Dear Dilemma:

No problems . . . more likely it will give a real boost to the proceedings. Since everyone will already be in a celebrating frame of mind, just carry the theme and spirit of the holiday to your wedding. Look over our five major Holiday themes for ready-made ideas on how to add a holiday fix to your wedding.

Q: Heaven knows, I'm devoted to candlelit dinners, Shakespearean plays, and fireflies in the night. Now that I'm to be married, how can I bring this same appealing quality to my wedding? I guess I'm just a . . .

—Hopeless Romantic

Dear Romantic:

Don't despair. Of course, any wedding is romantic, but for those extra whimsical touches, three themes quickly come to mind. These themes—Puck's Perfect Party, Light up the Night, and Romantic Renaissance— are sure to give you the kind of wedding your heart desires. You'll find suggestions for color schemes, favors, attendants' gifts, decorations, and floral bouquets that will satisfy your most romantic yearnings.

Q: Tell me if I'm wrong. Can't a small wedding be just as special as one with a large guest list?

—Right or Wrong

Dear Right:

Yes, you certainly are able to create wonderful memories with a small wedding. You'll see how several of the wedding themes can be adapted and used for the smaller wedding. For specific how-tos for small weddings, read the Daytime Informal theme and the At Home theme. You'll find you can have a memorable day with all the trimmings while avoiding the crush of a large crowd.

Q: The wedding date is set for my favorite time of year, spring. I think it would be nice to include some seasonal touches in the wedding setting. Can you help?

—Thinking Spring

Dear Spring:

It just happens that spring is my favorite season, too. In fact, I devoted a whole theme to this lighthearted time of year. You'll find fresh spring ideas for floral bouquets, pew markers, and centerpieces in the Spring Is Here theme. Since weddings are now popular year-round, I've given equal time to everybody. You'll find great ideas and plans for the other three seasons, as well.

Q: Our wedding guest list is made up of relatives and friends who expect and enjoy a creative party. Our wedding must be a major event!

—Uniquely Yours

Dear Uniquely:

You can start those creative juices flowing with ideas from any of the Timeless themes. If it's active drama your guests crave, select the

Medieval "Marry" Making theme. Or, turn to The Great Gatsby for a "novel' theme sure to please.

Q: It's true! We're headed for a magnificent honeymoon after the wedding. Would it be possible to start early and recreate the atmosphere of our destination at our reception?

—Honeymoon Bound

Dear Honeymoon:

If you can control your excitement long enough to read over the Destination themes, you should find a honey of an idea for your reception. There are five themes based on some of the top honeymoon destinations. Each theme will be sure to give your guests a taste of the wonderful vacation ahead of you.

Q: Weddings seem so wonderful until it's time to plan your own. There must be a logical way to go about doing a wedding.

—Looking for Answers

Dear Looking:

Planning a wedding is like building a house. You start from the ground up. Turn to the Wedding Plan List for a good step-by-step list of things to do before the wedding. You'll see, there's nothing like good preparation to soothe those jangled nerves!

Q: We want to show off our part of the country to the many out-of-town wedding guests who'll be coming. Is there a way to highlight our region at the wedding?

—Putting our Best Foot Forward

Dear Best Foot Forward:

The solution to your problem reminds me of the old adage "If the shoe fits, wear it!" In this case, if the region fits, use the theme. There are five Regional themes to look over, all with their own unique flavors, sights, and sounds. Choose the one that is closest to your homestead and let your guests savor the color of the area. Your guests will be sure to leave with fond memories of your wedding and your locale!

Q: When it rains, it pours. Our two daughters just announced their upcoming wedding dates . . . both in the same season. What to do?

—Almost Rained Out

Dear Almost:

Two weddings in one season are quite an undertaking. So you don't get caught in a monsoon, why not consider a double wedding? The Double Wedding theme shows you how to have one extraordinary wedding for two lovely couples. Your daughters will each have the chance to enjoy the spotlight, and you'll have two weddings for almost the price of one.

Q: We both enjoy the outdoors and want to exchange our vows in a beautiful outdoor scenic setting. Is this kind of wedding possible?

—Off the Beaten Track

Dear Beaten Track:

You're on the right track. Outdoor wedding sites are very popular especially in the warmer climes. Pick a favorite outdoor setting and then turn to the Scenic Setting theme or Lawn and Garden theme for the how-tos of making this site work for you. Everyone will enjoy the cathedral-like setting that nature has to offer.

Q: A small civil ceremony is planned. What kind of celebration is appropriate after the ceremony?

—Perplexed

Dear Perplexed:

Any celebration is suitable as long as it fits your style and taste. Look through the Civil Ceremony theme and discover the wide variety of choices you have to celebrate your marriage. Suggestions for wedding party dress as well as ceremony and reception sites are given, too. Enjoy yourself. This is going to be your big day.

Q: Everything is set for our wedding, except . . . I can't find the right bridal dress. You see, everything is going to be in the Victorian style, and I want to wear an authentic Victorian bridal dress.

—Victoria

Dear Victoria:

There is not a moment to lose. Turn to the Historical Dress Pattern Sources in the Fashion Guide to find names and addresses of companies that specialize in authentic historical dress patterns. You'll find a Victorian dress pattern in the companies' catalogs. Once you have the pattern, you or a dressmaker can easily sew the dress of your dreams. By the way, there are great ideas for decorating and entertaining in the Victorian manner in the Victorian Delight theme.

Q: My husband and I have a wonderful marriage, and we would like to celebrate our marriage and recite our vows—again. Are there any guidelines to follow?

—Encore

Dear Encore:

The reaffirmation ceremony is becoming more popular. Couples cite these reasons for wanting to reaffirm their vows: to strengthen their marriage, to enjoy the festive ceremony they missed the first time, or to celebrate a great marriage. Whatever the reason, this time around the only guidelines you have to follow is what makes the most sense to you. You'll find a variety of suggestions in the Reaffirmation theme to get you started on your wonderful day of renewal.

Q: I love the froth and frill of weddings, but how can I add a little dramatic spice to my wedding?

—Cool and Sophisticated

Dear Cool:

Try on the Contemporary Drama theme for a sensational wedding look. The focus on color for both dress and decorations should give your wedding the distinctive style you're searching for. Just pretend not to hear when your Aunt Sadie muses, "They don't make weddings like they used to."

Q: At the last wedding we attended, there was a delightful place favor for each guest at the reception. Do you have any good suggestions for favors that are a little different?

—Favorably Impressed

Dear Impressed:

Gifting your guests with favors adds to the loveliness of the day. Plenty of original and uncommonly good solutions can be found in the Favor Guide. If none of these suggestions work, perhaps a blending of two or more ideas will treat your guests right.

Q: Call it false pride, but I would like to see our wedding stand out from the crowd. Is our only solution to use the finest appointments?

—Soon to be Married

Dear Soon to Be:

Not at all. That's what makes themes for weddings so great! A wedding theme removes the need for lavish fixings and focuses on creativity. Have you ever noticed . . . creativity usually costs less and it's more fun? You can be confident that any of these fifty themes will ensure your wedding day happiness.

Decorative
2. Themes

These eye-catching themes are pretty, versatile, and easy to carry out. Choose the decorations that are most appealing to you, and create a beautiful, theme-inspired, wedding day.

PUCK'S PERFECT PARTY

Stunningly simple and sweet, you could say this theme comes straight from a midsummer night's dream. You'll see how wreaths of grapevine adorn tables, napkins, and your bridesmaids. Discover, too, how muted colors and live potted plants can turn a reception area into Puck's enchanted garden.

Choose your wedding colors from the soft peach, pink, and blue delphinium family for this fairyland delight. Bridesmaids should wear fresh flower circlets in their hair and carry grapevine wreaths. The wreaths are held slightly below the waist or down at the side. If you prefer a more traditional bouquet for yourself, select an all-white, loose cascade bouquet accented with ivy or fern.

Turn the reception area into a midsummer night's dream using live ferns and ivy planted in tubs. Add some garden flowers (delphiniums, hyacinths, pansies) to the tubs for extra color. If you water the soil well the night before or in the morning, the plants will be fresh all day. After the festivities, they can be brought to your house or given to your guests and planted in the garden.

To make the reception area a place of enchantment, hang softly playing wind chimes about. Engage a harpist or woodwind quartet to play lovely lyrical songs for additional magical, music notes.

Place grapevine wreaths flat at the center of each table. (Turn to Grapevine Wreath, Centerpiece Guide, to learn how to make a wreath of any size.) Arrange pillars of different-sized candles in the center of the wreath and tuck reindeer moss into the cracks and crannies of your arrangement. You'll find reindeer moss at your florist. The moss resembles a ball-shaped white sponge and can be moistened and formed into any shape you need. Set small glass vases filled with sweet peas, alstroemeria, or iris in and around the arrangement.

Each place setting should be a part of the theme, as well. Slip miniature grapevine rings around peach, pink, or blue napkins. Then set small packages of sweet pea seeds above the napkins. Attach a small note to each package that says something like this: "Thank you for favoring us with your presence at our celebration. Plant these seeds for their sweet fragrance and as a memory of this occasion."

Circle the wedding cake with a grapevine wreath, too. Accent the vines with ivy and narrow white ribbons.

When the festivities begin, gift your attendants with a theme-related thank-you. Give each attendant a one-of-a-kind, hand-blown glass goblet. The ethereal quality of the goblets will be enjoyed and admired throughout the day. Contact your local vocational school first for hand-blown glass sources. Students often have quality work available for sale.

As you can see, simple efforts will lead to a fantasy-come-true. This dream of a wedding is certain to have you and Puck sharing a secret smile together

BALLOON BASH

Rise to the occasion of your wedding with balloons as your main decorating element. You'll find that balloons bridge the gaps between ages, sexes, races, religions, and cultures. Once you've chosen your colors, you'll be off to a flying start.

Wedding balloons are usually white, silver, or clear with confetti. In some areas you can find clear balloons filled with small balloons in your choice of wedding colors.

Decorate your church or temple with arches of balloons across every fourth row of pews. (See Balloon Tips, in Decorations for the Reception Guide.) Attach the balloon arches to the pews with white satin bows. Since balloon arches are a bit tricky, you may need the help of balloon professionals for this decorating step.

You can, however, easily pot clusters of three to five helium-fill balloons or balloons on sticks in foil-wrapped flowerpots. Set the potted balloons at the sanctuary, entrances, and any empty spots at the reception area. Vary the height of the balloons as needed.

Balloons can also substitute for rice as a symbol of good wishes for the couple. On an agreed-upon cue, everyone releases a helium balloon when the couple emerges from the church or temple. This festive lift-off can be arranged as the couple leaves the reception, too.

Or, perhaps you would rather have a "balloon drop" at the reception. In this case, you can rent shower nets and fill the net with balloons. Fill these "drop" balloons with air instead of helium so they will fall rather than rise when released.

Talk to your florist about combining balloons and floral centerpieces. You'll get more punch for your money with the added height of the balloons. The eye will be drawn to the balloons, down to the floral arrangement and on to the complete table setting. Tie slim 1/10-inch ribbons to the necks of the balloons and let them curl downward naturally.

Experiment with several ideas for maximum balloon saturation. Highlight bottles of champagne and sparkling water with balloons and ribbons. Favor your guests with packets of netting filled with mints the same color as the balloons. Just for fun, attach a balloon to each packet.

Finally, include balloons in a sincere thank-you to Mom and Dad. Give them an appropriately worded balloon saying "Super Dad" or "Super Mom." Your parents will enjoy this public display of your affection.

This theme is restricted only by the imagination. As they say in balloon circles, the sky is the limit.

GIFTS FROM THE SEA

Pearls, exquisite pearls, are the main contributors to this grand design. Yet other decorative Neptune ideas will demand a certain pay-attention level from your guests, too. Make one promise, though . . . no mermaids!

This theme is fairly simple. Look at every element of your wedding day to see how you can add some reminder of the sea. Let's begin with the invitations. You might choose invitations printed with a shell and a verse reminding you of the sea. A good source for quotations is Anne Morrow Lindbergh's book, "Gift from the Sea."

Now, on to your dress and accessories. Pearls come easily to mind. For instance, bridal dresses and headpieces are often decorated with seed pearls. And you can accessorize your costume with a pearl necklace and earrings.

Your florist can suggest ways to add pearls to the bridal party bouquets. Pearl sprays (pearls strung on a monofilament strand) make graceful fill-ins for bouquets. If you've been given a strand of heirloom pearls, whether from your grandmother or someone else, have the pearls worked into your bouquet of flowers.

In this case, attendants' gifts, which can sometimes be hard to find, are a simple matter. Select pearl earrings for the bridesmaids and mother-of-pearl cuff links for the groom and his attendants. The pearl accessories are a thoughtful gift and are yet another addition to your theme.

Create a centerpiece that is a little different from the usual floral bouquet for this theme. Set fishbowls in the center of a tray of shells. Use simulated pearls instead of rock in the bottom of the bowls, and drape strands of pearls from willow branches down into the fishbowl. Add one or two small fish to the bowl. (For complete directions, see Gifts from the Sea Centerpiece, in the Centerpiece Guide.)

The sweetest seaside additions to this theme are the favors for your guests. Collect or buy medium-sized seashells, enough for each place setting. Clean the shells first, then write or paint your names and date of marriage on each shell. Set chocolate truffles, seashell shaped, in each shell. Cover the shell and truffles with cling wrap. Gather the ends of the wrap together with a white ribbon and finish off with a bow.

You may choose this theme because it happens to evoke special memories of a seaside meeting, a yachting weekend, or a beachside proposal. However, the simple elegance of this theme is reason enough to use it on this day of special days.

FANFARE

"FAN-tastic" is the operative word for this theme. Highlight your wedding with fans . . . old and new, large and small, paper and linen. Decoratively speaking, they're easy to use and hard to beat. Enjoy these fan ideas, enough here to fill your entire wedding day.

Combine a pretty fan with flowers and ribbons for an unusual wedding bouquet treatment. Ask your florist to trim the fan (provided by you or the florist) with white gardenias or orchids. When it's time to throw the bouquet to your single friends, detach the flowers and keep the fan for your memory box. Some brides have second bouquets made for the sole purpose of having a keepsake after throwing the bouquet to their friends.

Bridesmaids' bouquets should have the same shape and the fan should be used in the same way as in the bridal bouquet. Vary the color of the flowers so each bouquet has its own special look.

Use fans, again, to mark the guests' pews. Decorate the fans with a signature flower from your floral bouquets, and add asparagus fern and ribbons. You can sometimes find fans with florist foam already attached at local craft stores. Lacking the florist foam, simply wire the flowers to the fan and then to the pew. Wrap florist tape around the wire first to prevent the wire from damaging the pews.

As a way of introducing your theme, choose fan-related invitations. Design your own invitations if none are available. Can't draw a straight line? Then find a creative friend who can, or find a picture of a fan that you like and computer scan it. Be aware of copyright laws. Printers cannot print anything that is a copy right unless they have signed permission. The printer than can use the artwork or a computer scan for the invitations, and, if you wish, for paper napkins, and ceremony programs, as well.

Besides using fans with flowers for the centerpieces (your florist can help you with this), fold the napkins into the fan fold. This napkin fold lends itself to a pre-wedding, napkin-folding party. Once the napkins are folded, it is a simple matter to place them at each place setting on the day of the wedding. If your reception is held at a hotel, restaurant, or country club, the service people may know how to do this fold. (Follow the instructions for the Fan Fold in the Table Setting Guide.)

Favor your guests with fans, too. Purchase small paper fans from an import shop. Print your names and the date of your wedding on the fan itself or on the handle. Use a fine point marking pen in a color that contrasts with the paper.

This theme suggests gifts for the wedding attendants, as well. Give antique fans or decorative wall fans. Engrave small brass medallions with your names and wedding date and fasten to the fan's handle with decorative chain or ribbon. A short note with the fan, such as the following, adds sentimental value to the gift: "Now that the FANfare is almost over, we want to thank you for helping our FANtasy come true. It will always be a FANtastic event in our memory!"

You'll transform your wedding day into a well-thought-out event with some or all of these fan-related ideas. The attention to detail will create a truly personal and creative wedding.

Parasol Style

If you've chosen parasols to complement yur wedding day dresses, you can develop a complete theme around this decorative accessory.

By all means, use flowers, ribbons, and bows, too. But keep the parasol, as your signature piece, evident throughout the wedding day.

Start the parasol planning the right way by selecting invitations sporting a perky parasol. Repeat the parasol on any enclosures, as well. If you can't find a parasol design in the sample book at your local stationer, turn to mail-order catalogs. You'll need to place your order at least three months before the wedding, so begin your shopping well before the wedding.

Should your bridesmaids balk at carrying parasols, ask your florist to tuck a miniature lace parasol in the bouquets. Add some flowers to the parasol you will be carrying. Tie a narrow ribbon (1/16-inch) and a small bow to the top of the parasol. Drape more lengths of the same ribbon from the top and add tiny flowers tied to the ribbon with love knots.

Switch to umbrellas when gifting your attendants. You have a choice of fun-and-fancy rain umbrellas, businesslike telescoping umbrellas, just-for-fun beach or golf umbrellas, or even those sporting-event headbands that support a tiny umbrella.

Then back to parasols to add charm to the reception. Collect paper, lace, or silk parasols, enough to place one parasol on each table. Fill the upside-down parasol with a dried flower arrangement of heather and baby's breath. Add a few silk flowers to this arrangement for extra color. Since you are using an arrangement that doesn't need water to stay fresh, you won't have to worry about water stains on the parasols.

Finish the arrangement with dainty, picot-edged ribbons. Tie the ribbons to the parasol handle, letting the ends fall gracefully down to the flower arrangement. Use any color ribbon except iridescent. Dried flowers and iridescent colors don't work well together.

Continue the parasol look with these easy-to-find parasol party accessories.

Tuck tiny lace or paper cocktail parasols into the folds of the napkins or tie to the napkins with ribbon and lace.

Accent each place setting with lace plastic parasols tipped upside down. Fill with color-coordinated wedding mints.

Select from a variety of enchanting parasol cake tops, usually featuring a handpainted couple standing under a lace parasol surrounded by tiers of lace and white satin.

Finally choose a large lace or honeycomb tissue parasol to mark the gift-gathering spot. Prop it up umbrella fashion or stand the parasol upright. To stand, pop the parasol handle into an enamel designer bag and fill with light sand or birdseed. Loosely wrap the top of the bag around the handle with ribbon and bow. Decorate the handle with flowers and twine narrow ribbons from the top, letting the ribbons fall naturally.

This parasol theme will hint at grace and gentility on your wedding day. Yet the props you need are inexpensive and not hard to find. As easy as this theme is to carry out, it will truly convey a romantic charm that will be long remembered.

LIGHT UP THE NIGHT

Candlelight and romance go together like love and marriage. In this theme, candles play an important symbolic role during the ceremony, as well as providing a soft romantic mood throughout the wedding festivities. Use plenty of candles and dim the lights. Evening, of course, is best for this theme.

Light up the night with candles everywhere. Line the walkway to the entrance of your ceremony and reception area with luminarias. Luminarias are inexpensive and easy to make. Cut out patterns of flowers or snowflakes on the sides of lunch-size paper bags. Fill the bags with about 2 inches of sand or cat litter and roll the tops to make a cuff. Anchor a votive or plumber's candle (found at hardware stores) in the sand, and set the bags at intervals the length of the walkway.

Rather than ordering floral arrangements for the ceremony, focus on quantities of candles. Make them festive with ribbon and bows. In some cases, churches or synagogues have pew tapers yc during the ceremony. Pew tapers are candleholders th pews and are used for special occasions.

The candle can play an important role during the ceremony as well. The sharing of a lifetime together is symbolized with the traditional lighting of a unity candle. The bride and groom light this candle simultaneously during the ceremony to signify their newly joined lives.

Before designing your candle arrangements for the reception area, check first with the management. Fire regulations may prohibit use of an open flame. Once you do have the go-ahead, collect candles and anything that glitters, shines, or reflects. You'll double your decorative impact with mirrors, glitter, rhinestones, and opalescent ribbons arranged to reflect the flicker of the candles.

Mirror squares, available from most lumber stores, make excellent bases for centerpieces. Set groupings of candles on the squares and wind opalescent ribbon in and around the candles. Scatter glitter and rhinestones over all. Arrange smaller centerpieces to set at intervals on the tables or design one large centerpiece for each table. Check to make sure the flame isn't at eye level of your seated guests.

Once the festivities are over, your personal attendant or a parent can collect the candle stubs. Then, when you have time, melt the stubs and mold them into one large candle. Decorate with wedding memorabilia such as an imprinted paper napkin, an invitation, or a wedding snapshot. This special memory candle can be used at your first anniversary celebration and subsequent celebrations.

Favor your guests and gift your attendants with candles, too. Purchase white candles and tie with ribbons in your wedding colors. Personalize the attendants' candles with initialed candleholders.

Whether you wish to celebrate your wedding on the longest day of the year or just enjoy the enchantment of a candlelit evening, this theme will cast a warm glow on the proceedings anytime.

3. Style Setting Themes

Your wedding can be a stylish trendsetter whether it's traditional or innovative. Pick the theme that says it's *you,* and enjoy the wonderful ambience throughout your wedding day.

CASUAL CHIC

Strictly stylish, from the wedding party dresses to the favor each guest receives, this theme has flair. Handpainted flowers, personalized attendants' gifts, and striking centerpieces are a few of the features. Yes, it's a little time consuming, but you'll create a wedding that is elegant and uniquely yours.

Personal elegance can be yours with an individualized approach to your bridesmaids' dresses. Stencil or airbrush the birthday flower of each bridesmaid directly on the dress fabric. Create one, large, perfect blossom or a border of flowers edging the hem. Fabric painting can be used on off-the-rack dresses as well as on home-sewn dresses.

Your bridal dress can be individualized in this way, too. Design a small rose, or any favorite flower, for your veil or the hem of your dress. Fill in the design with white puff paint. Puff paint expands, leaving a white-on-white puffy effect much like a swiss dot. If you decide to try your hand at fabric painting, read the list of hints found in Fabric Painting Hints, in the Fashion Guide.

Elegant and unique do not necessarily mean expensive. Look for small but exquisite personal items to express your thanks to your attendants. Select soft leather or tortoiseshell-covered address book for the men on your list and lovely, floral-covered address books for the bridesmaids. Then personalize each gift by applying their initials in gold or silver on the cover.

Plan a leisurely luncheon or sit-down dinner amid soft music and delightful table appointments. Make simple but eye catching arrangements of iris, snapdragon, star-of-Bethlehem, and freesia that can be arranged gracefully in floral foam set in a silver or gold plastic saucer.

Accent the spray of flowers with silver or gold onion grass. Onion grass comes wired to a picklike stick and its ribbonlike strands spring out in a fountain effect. Pull the strands taut as if you were working with a curling, wrapping gift ribbon for a loose curl effect. If onion grass isn't available, you can use silver mylar ribbon. Mylar ribbon is used to tie balloons, so you should be able to find it at party supply stores.

Wedding Ring Kisses (See Wedding Ring Kisses in the Decorative Recipe Guide) wrapped in metallic mylar wrapping paper will pick up the gold or silver of the onion grass in the centerpieces. Favor everyone with these kisses. After the candy is dropped from the spoon, but before it hardens, place tiny wedding rings on the tip of the candy swirl. (You'll find rings at wedding or party supply stores.) When the candy is ready, wrap these tasteful treats individually.

A signature tablecloth allows your guests to become personally involved in your wedding memories. Drape a lace-edged tablecloth next to the guest book with a textile pen and a request for your guests' signatures. Later, work these names, the date of your wedding, and any decorative flourishes with embroidery floss.

Chic is a matter of developing an elegant but easy personal style. This theme lends support to this effort. If you succeed, you'll have the satisfaction of a fashionable, one-of-a-kind wedding celebration.

LLY YOURS

a traditional white wedding? From wedding dress to irowing, you can depend on the traditions found in this theme to fulfill your most cherished dreams. Moreover, you'll discover the reasons behind each ritual and custom.

Everyone knows that white is the traditional bridal color. In Roman times, the wearing of white signified a time of celebration. But did you know that it was Americans with their newly acquired wealth who introduced the custom of wearing white bridal dresses? It was a way to display their wealth. Only the wealthy could afford to buy a white dress to be worn on only one occasion.

The attendants' attire, often similar in style to the bride and groom, is rooted in the custom of warding off evil curses from the couple. In early times, friends and family wore the same clothes as the wedding couple in order to fool potential evil-wishers and deflect any curse on the marriage.

Today, the bride's attendants traditionally wear a color of the bride's choosing. The male attendants follow the groom's dress lead. However, their ties and cummerbunds often complement the dress of the bridesmaid they are escorting.

The bridal bouquet has an early history, too. Bouquets of rosemary and garlic were often carried by brides in early Roman times. It was said that the herbs would drive away evil spirits. Later, flowers chosen for their meaning, such as roses for eternal love and ivy for fidelity, replaced the strong-smelling herb bouquets.

Brides today, treasure white flowers for their bouquets. Freesia, lily of the valley, stephanotis, Queen Anne's lace, and roses are popular choices. (White flowers begin to wilt and show brown spots sooner, so discuss the hardiness of each flower with your florist.)

An abundance of flowers has traditionally symbolized a life of plenty for the wedding couple. For that reason, you'll find several bouquets of flowers in the chapel or synagogue and in the reception area of today's wedding.

The cake cutting ceremony, another tradition, was born long ago. It is said that a flat wheat bread was broken over the early Roman bride's head to ensure the couple's luck and fertility. In the Middle Ages, the wedding couple were to kiss over a pile of little cakes. If the cakes fell, the guests would pelt the unfortunate couple with the cakes and then eat the crumbs.

Today, the bride and groom, with arms interlocked, cut a piece from the wedding cake and offer a bit of cake to each other. This symbolizes their promise to share the future together.

Another must at the traditional wedding are Jordan almonds, sometimes called confetti. Often the almonds are wrapped in netting and tied with ribbon. Symbolically, these favors represent the bitterness of life (the almonds) offset with the sweetness of love (candy coating).

Yet another tradition is rice throwing. As a symbolic gesture, throwing rice (birdseed is rapidly replacing rice) at the couple is supposed to bestow abundance on the newlyweds and good luck on the guests.

This theme is true to wedding customs that are observed in countless weddings. But remember—wedding traditions from eons ago don't have to be followed today. Your family traditions have a place in your wedding, too. Include meaningful family traditions as well as the time-honored rituals, and you'll create a truly personalized, tradition-filled day.

I LOVE COUNTRY

If you're the type who loves country and plans to decorate your home with country furnishings, you'll want to adopt this look for your wedding plans, as well. Homespun crafts, colorful prints, and down-home music are teamed up to create an inviting setting. Besides having a warm, comfortable feeling, this look is easy to adapt to any kind of accommodations.

The country look begins with the bride's and bridesmaids' attire. Accessorize an ivory satin and lace, country-style wedding dress with crocheted gloves and a cluster bouquet of flowers backed with a lace holder. Bridesmaid dresses are in earth-tone colors. Prints are appropriate. Straw hats and cluster bouquets complete the country look.

Gift your bridesmaids with cream crocheted gloves to complement their gowns and enhance the country look. Give the groom's attendants white handkerchiefs embroidered with their initials as their thank-you gifts.

The ideal site for your wedding ceremony? A small country church. You'll find getting to the church on time decidedly uncomplicated because of less traffic and you'll enjoy a wonderful setting once you're there.

Whether or not your ceremony is held in a country church, you can still create a country feeling for your ceremony with a wedding quilt. Drape it across your kneeling bench or hang it in the background as a banner.

You can create this elegant quilt by using squares of fabric from your dress and the bridesmaids' dresses and joining the pieces together with backing material in your favorite color. A more detailed quilt can be made with the help of your friends and relatives. Ask them to needlework a meaningful design on a muslin square you send to each of them. Then you can work a center square with your names and wedding date.

This quilt can help you create the same country feeling at the reception. Casually drape the quilt across the gift table, next to the guest book, or hang it on the wall behind the head table.

Another way to achieve a country look at the reception is to use straw hats as centerpieces. Place a straw hat on the dining table and fill the rim of the hat with daisies, zinnias, and strawflowers. Tie ribbon around the band of the hat and trail the streamers to the place settings.

Special little paperweight favors for each place setting can be crafted easily. Find smooth rocks, about the size that will fit in the palm of your hand, and paint them in country colors. These paperweights can then be decorated with tiny painted flowers and inscribed with the message "THINK HAPPY," along with your names and wedding date.

Because this is a classic country theme, arrange for country-style entertainment. Fiddle or banjo music will start feet tapping to the tunes, sure to please for dining enjoyment and a great filler at intermission time. Square dancing is a must after dining. You can't find a better mixer, and it's fun for all ages.

All in all, this theme is meant to generate old-fashioned country hospitality. Best of all, it will create a warm, happy memory for years to come.

Sentimental Reasons

A wedding is a time for sentiment. Whether you choose to remember weddings past or add meaningful touches of your own, it's easy to fill this day with sentimental symbolism. This theme will get you started thinking of how you can add special moments and memories to your wedding day.

Focus your attention on one of the easiest areas to create sentimental impact—the wedding dress. It can be your mother's wedding dress, perhaps altered slightly, or a new version that's a better fit for you but still styled like your mother's dress. Then, in keeping with something borrowed, wear your sister's bridal veil. Something old could be a grandmother's broach.

Work with the bridal bouquet if the wedding dress isn't available. Find a photograph of your mother's bouquet and have the florist design a copy of the bouquet. Another idea might feature special flowers in your bouquet such as the pink roses that were given to you on your first date. Add more sentiment by using your grandmother's heirloom handkerchief in the bouquet.

For sentimental value, use the same solo sung at your parents' wedding as a feature of your ceremony. Some couples choose a medley of songs—songs important to them through their courtship days—to be played before the ceremony.

Pictures are always an important part of weddings. So bring out all the studio pictures of your family's weddings and arrange them in a special gallery set up just for picture showing. You may prefer to arrange one large collage of the extended family wedding pictures.

Another approach is to set up a gallery of "his" and "hers" growing-up years or a picture history of your courtship days. If you have the necessary equipment, make all the pictures into slides for a special continuous slide show, set to music.

Of course you'll be adding to the collection of wedding pictures during your wedding. Here's one way to create a whole different look for your wedding album memories. Hand out inexpensive or disposable cameras to the young set in the crowd. You'll be assured of a unique pictorial perspective of your wedding. The kids will have fun, too.

You'll find that the things friends and family do for you on this happy day have sentimental value, too. Don't be shy. Give them a chance to say yes or no to a special request. Then, during the wedding day, acknowledge any special flower arranging, hair setting, table decorating, and so on, to let everyone know how much you cherish their personal touches.

Keep looking for ways to add personal touches, unique to you and your family, as you make your way through the wedding plans. Let the ideas in this theme give you a gentle nudge toward the start of a singularly happy and sentiment filled day.

CONTEMPORARY DRAMA

The thing that makes this theme appear so contemporary is the colors used on the wedding day . . . or rather, the lack of color. Black and white, only, is the unifying thread tying together invitations, decorations, and costumes.

Extend your invitations to this gala in a modern print style, black ink on white paper. Ask your stationer to show you the available contemporary print styles. Before mailing the invitation, insert a request to your guests to wear black and white attire only. Dress can range from casual daytime apparel to after-six wear, depending on how formal you want your wedding to be.

This black-and-white color theme is highlighted by the wedding party dress and bouquets. Bridesmaids should carry white cascade bouquets in sharp contrast to their elegant black dresses. Their bouquets should include rubrum lilies, star-of-Bethlehem, and freesia. The men in the wedding party should wear black tuxedos or suits and white shirts. Tuck white freesia into their lapels.

You should wear a traditional white gown and carry a larger version of the bridesmaids' cascade bouquet. Complement the white rubrum lilies and freesia with green ivy and lemon leaves.

The table settings, too, should reflect the black-and-white color scheme. Arrange all white floral centerpieces in black containers. Set tall, elegant candles around each centerpiece. The 15-inch to 18-inch-long candles are assuming bestseller status, so you should find them easily. Set flowers and candles on a white tablecloth with white napkins. Fold the napkins into a roll and tie with a black and white ribbon, striped or dotted. Use the same ribbon to tie decorative bows around the candle holders and the centerpieces.

You can offer some very contemporary party favors to your guests that accentuate the black-and-white theme. In place of Jordan almonds, offer licorice pieces. Put a spoonful of licorice into squares of white netting. Tie the netting into a bag with a narrow black ribbon.

Another possible party favor is small (two-glass serving size) bottles of champagne. One brand of champagne is conveniently bottled in black glass and foil. Tie a white satin ribbon around the neck of each bottle.

A wedding cake of alternate layers of chocolate and white cake is perfect for the contemporary black and white theme. An all-chocolate cake with white frosting is another choice. Trim either cake with fresh white flowers and green ivy.

For sheer decorative drama, this theme is hard to beat. A certain elegant mood is established reflecting a distinctive, contemporary style. If you've always been on the cutting edge of fashion, you'll have no problem featuring black as a major, decorative wedding color.

4. Regional Themes

S etting the scene, regional style, gives your guests a taste of authentic U.S.A. These themes will allow your guests to savor the unique flavor and color of your region.

NORTHEAST REGION

Since the spirit of '76 prevails in this part of the country, you will be able to arrange a happy blend of colonial history and celebration. Chances are, you live close to a historic site that is open to the public. If so, then it's simply a matter of enhancing the colonial ambience by attending to the menu, decorations, and gift details. It'll be a day of historic splendor to remember.

But first, the success of this theme depends on finding historic sites for all or some of the traditional wedding day activities. Look in the telephone book and call the historical society, local chamber of commerce, department of parks and recreation, and the department of tourism. Ask about the availability of ceremony and reception locations. Your ceremony could be held in a university chapel, a country church, or a botanical garden of special historical significance, and your reception could be given in a historical inn or hotel.

Let accessories like the wedding party bouquets support the colonial look. A favorite bouquet in those days was a tussie mussie, a cluster of flowers and herbs. Update this bouquet by tying tiny lace potpourri packages to the streamers and choosing daisies and carnations for the flowers.

Even transportation from ceremony to reception, usually an ordinary matter, can be returned into a colonial event with a horse-drawn carriage. Treat the whole wedding party or just yourselves to this nostalgic ride. Picture taking is a must.

When you select a reception site, preferably a historic inn or hotel, try to find out if the staff will be serving in Early American costume. This gives you more ambience for the money. Also, don't assume that because the inn is historic, you'll be served in a room that has the proper amount of historical flavor. Check for yourself.

Once you've decided on the reception area, start planning the table centerpieces. Collect pewter pieces and antique glassware such as cruets, sugar and creamers, or cups and saucers. Fill them with fresh flowers. Unmatched pieces are fine as long as the flowers are similar in color.

As for wedding favors for your guests, treat everyone to a small box of saltwater taffy. Besides tasting good, the taffy is representative of the Northeast. Display the candy in a clear, plastic box to show off its many flavors and colors. Tie a brightly colored ribbon around the box and set one favor at each place setting.

Pewter is very popular in this area, as well. Pewter picture frames, bracelets, cordials, or beer steins make great attendant gifts.

Creating an Early American setting for this theme demonstrates a variety of good things this region has to offer. You'll find that going back in time to colonial days is a sure way to add flavor and atmosphere to your wedding.

SOUTH REGION

Evoke a Southern mood on your wedding day. Simply select the flowers and greenery that grow plentifully in the South and combine these with gracious Southern traditions.

English ivy, a symbol of fidelity, is used frequently in Southern decorating because of its availability. Substitute baskets of ivy trimmed with ribbon for bouquets of flowers in the ceremony area. Tie strands of ivy accented with ribbon to the pews. If allowed, attach ivy-filled, reed half-baskets to the entrance doors.

For your wedding party bouquets, choose a traditional Southern Williamsburg look. Bouquet-in-a-cloud, a longtime favorite, is a rounded cluster of flowers with netting nestled over the flowers. Net bags of potpourri are knotted to the end of the bouquet's ribbons. Use flowers available in the South for your bridal bouquet. Magnolia, freesia, gardenia, or stephanotis—the choice is yours.

Make good use of the Williamsburg, Della Robbia look in your reception area. For centerpieces, pyramid fruit in glass or brass compotes or trays. Top the pyramid of fruit with a small pineapple, a sign of Southern welcome and hospitality. (See Della Robbia Centerpiece in the Centerpiece Guide.) Complete the centerpiece with slender tapers grouped around the pyramid of fruit.

Carry the Della Robbia look to each individual place setting. Highlight linen napkins with Della Robbia, papier mâché fruit usually found as tree decorations at Christmastime. Wrap the wired end of the fruit around each rolled napkin.

Above each napkin, place small favors of Marzipan candy shaped into a variety of fruits. Marzipan candy is a confection of ground almonds, sugar, and egg white made into a paste. Fill small white boxes with the candy and tie with ribbon. Fashion a pretty bow on top.

Tiny gold pineapple charms, engraved with the date of the wedding, appropriately solves the wedding party gift problem. The charms can later be attached to wristwatches, bracelets, or chains. A short explanation of the tradition of the pineapple symbolizing hospitality will make the gift more meaningful.

It's traditional in the South and elsewhere to have guests sign a guest book for the couple. Choose an elegant white book of white or cream-colored pages with your names and wedding date embossed on the cover. Place the book at a prominent spot in your reception area, or volunteer some of the younger members of the family to take the book around to the guests.

This theme is in keeping with the Southern tradition of charm and grace. It's pretty. It's traditional. Everyone, whether from the North, South, East, or West, will enjoy this taste of the regional South.

MIDWEST REGION

Looking for a good mixture of down-home sociability and celebration? Then let the Midwest influence your wedding day choices. You'll find plenty of ideas to celebrate.

Picture the colors of vibrant, growing plants (green), the ripening of grain and wheat(cream), and the voluptuousness of rich earth (brown). Adapt these colors for your own and use them with some variation throughout the day. Creamy white, of course, works for the bridal dress, pale mint green to dark hunter green for the bridesmaids' dresses. Inject a drop of color from the opposite end of the spectrum by choosing bouquets of red, orange, and yellow blossoms.

Order one or two floral bouquets for the sanctuary, but use free-form sprays of dried grasses for the pew markers. Tie the sprays to the pews with a 3-inch width of brown, cream, and green plaid ribbon. (See Attaching Pew Markers, in the Decorations for the Ceremony Guide for the best way to attach the sprays of dried grass to the pews.)

During the summer and fall, you can find grasses that are free for the picking. Stop at any roadside or empty lot, and you'll come away with armloads of bouquet material.

Fill wicker baskets with arrangements of grasses for the reception area, too. Follow two simple rules for successful dried grass arrangements: Tie bunches of grass together and group varying heights in one container. Don't fill a container with more than three different varieties of grasses. Finish the arrangements with a flourish of ribbons and bows.

Table favors come alive with the aroma of fresh, baked bread, another Midwest influence. Stencil each loaf of bread with small hearts. Arrange one loaf per basket along with a tiny jar of preserves. Tuck a personalized wedding napkin in the package and wrap tightly with plastic wrap. (See Stenciled Bread, Decorative Recipe Guide, for how to stencil bread.)

Just as love is to marriage, so coffee is to breakfast time in the Midwest. Give your attendants coffee mugs their names printed on the side, and tuck in a freshly ground gourmet coffee. Gift wrap it in the same kind of basket used for the favors.

Usually a band is booked for the guests' dancing enjoyment, or a disc jockey is hired to play records or tapes. In either case, don't assume that all the requests will be filled. Make a list ahead of time that includes ethnic dances, the lindy, and current dance music.

Sometime during the dancing, another tradition is observed. That is the dollar dance. Simply put, the men line up and pay a dollar for the privilege of dancing with the bride. The same is true in reverse, with the women dancing with the groom Someone—attendants or a friend—collect the dollars and directs the proceedings until the couple has danced with everyone in line.

Whether this wedding takes place in the Midwest or is given for the sake of Midwestern guests, there are several ideas featured in this theme to make everyone feel at home. Hugs and kisses are required, and warm fuzzies are freely given and accepted.

Northwest Region

Once you've been to the Northwest, you'll never forget the sights and flavors of the region. Here in the Pacific Rim states, snow-topped mountains, fish-inhabited waterways, and flower-scented gardens are enjoyed and celebrated. You can bring some of this bounty from the outdoors in large or small doses to your wedding.

Perfume the air in your church or temple with bouquets of fir or cedar. Fashion a branch of evergreen trimmed with metallic gold ribbon and fasten (See Attaching Pew Markers, Decorations for the Ceremony Guide) to every third pew. Use the same metallic ribbon to trim the white candles.

Repeat the green, white, and gold theme in your table settings. Drape a table covered in white linen with garlands of pine roping studded with gold metallic bows. Layer flat cedar on the center of the table and add silver-tipped fir. Nestle votive candles in c ·~·l··-polys among the fir branches, and sprinkle gold-glitzed pin· about the centerpiece.

For other interesting points on the table, tie the · cones and a tiny spray of cedar to white napkins, bu·

the pine cones a glitzy gold. Add a handful of cones to a small basket, add a pinch of glitter, top with a bow, and set at each place setting. Give nature a hand by sprinkling a favorite fragrance such as pine scent on the cones. Guests can use these fragranced cone favors for coffee table or fireplace aroma. Cover the baskets with transparent cling wrap for convenient take-home gifts.

Use the menu to reflect the region's taste treats. A sampling of crab, salmon, and halibut will demonstrate the richness of the Northwest's waters besides being just plain good.

Run garlands of pine roping tied with gold metallic ribbon bows along any arches and entryway. Add strings of tiny white lights as a welcome highlight. You can decorate the gift and cake table with the same garlands. Top the wedding cake with a representation of a favorite outdoor activity, such as skiing or boating.

For those who want a picturesque wedding site, everything from ski lodges to yachts is available. Dash off to the sites in motor launches or horse-drawn sleighs for an extra filip of fun.

The wedding site can inspire creative ideas for gifting your attendants. If a wintry site, consider sleigh bells hanging from a decorative ribbon. A site on or near the water? Miniature crafted ships or boats personalized with their names and the wedding date could be an attendant gift answer.

If you think of plans for your wedding day as a recipe and the seasoning choice as yours, then what a wide variety of taste this theme offers. Pick and choose those Northwest seasonings that will demonstrate the best the region has to offer.

SOUTHWEST REGION

Here's a theme that shares all the warmth and color of the Southwest. Take your color theme from the sunset and accessorize with decorative reminders of the area. Activities might mean rodeo-style entertainment, Western dancing, or playing in the ~at outdoors.

As for special sites, you have a wide variety of choices. The Southwest offers mountaintops, desert locales, working ranches, renovated ghost towns, settler missions, and movie locations. Pick your site and enjoy.

Wherever you choose to have your reception, terra cotta dishes, colorful Indian-style blankets, and drip-hardened candles will tell of design elements typical of the Southwestern area. These elements show off best when used in unexpected ways. For example, angle the blankets casually across the tables or hang them over an occasional chair back. Set terra cotta flowerpots and saucers on the table as utensil holders and food servers. Stand centerpiece candles tall in terra cotta crocks filled with gravel and fit cactus plants snugly in terra cotta planters. You can find interesting terra cotta pieces in garden centers.

Sculpturelike folded napkins are always fun, especially when the folded napkin fits well with the theme. Tuck Cactus Fold napkins in chunky glassware. (See Cactus Fold, Table Setting Guide, for directions.) Use plain, square napkins in desert colors.

Finally, to complete the table setting, set small but interesting pots of cactus at each place setting. After the party is over, your guests can take them home as keepsakes of your wedding. Personalize the gifts by printing your names and the date of the wedding on the pots.

Accent this desert ambience with plantings of brilliant bougainvillea and hibiscus. Rent or purchase, keeping in mind that these plants can be transplanted later in your garden. Don't overlook nonfloral accents that are traditionally Southwest. Feature tin lampshades, bleached cattle skulls, or Indian pottery. Try to choose items that work in harmony. Just as you carefully choose your decorations to blend with your theme, select your attendants' gifts to fit the occasion. A sampling of gifts distinctive to the Southwest might include a terra cotta sun, turquoise jewelry, real or simulated, a geometric sun catcher with the date of your wedding etched on the glass, and so on.

This theme can be adapted to elegant or casual tastes with no trouble at all. Either way, your wedding day will express the best of what the Southwest has to offer.

5. Timeless Themes

Looking for a way to capture your guests' attention and stir the imagination? Then consider reenacting scenes from yesteryear. These themes create a grand photograph of days past that invites everyone to join in the spirit of your wedding day.

MEDIEVAL "MARRY" MAKING

This theme, borrowed from the court life of the Middle Ages, is full of boisterous good cheer. As the wedding couple, you will preside over this merrymaking court. Everything will be in royal good form, from invitations to the last mandolin tune. So sound the bugles and let this wedding day begin! Invitations to this merry affair should represent the grand court manner. Compose the invitation in the Old English style, and print or write in calligraphy on parchment paper. Then seal the envelopes using wax and a sealing impression.

Create a little bit of Camelot for yourself with a Medieval-design wedding dress. Look for patterns showing a heavy satin, floor length gored skirt. Fortunately, a handful of designers and pattern makers create dresses based on fashions of previous centuries. (See Historical Dress Pattern Sources, Fashion Guide, for addresses of costume pattern companies.) Complement your Medieval dress by wearing a wreath of fresh flowers, just as the maidens did in the Middle Ages.

Another way to achieve a sense of medieval court life is to place live medieval "statues" in the reception area. Rent actors from the local high school, college, or summer theater group for the day and dress them as characters from the Middle Ages. A tavern maid, a court jester, and a dashing duke are all you need. Standing motionless among the guests let them come to life every so often. A sudden buss on the cheek from the dashing duke, perhaps a juggling feat from the jester, or a sly wink from the tavern maid will get things going.

Create table settings worthy of King Author's court. Cover the tables with white table linens to serve as a neutral background for multicolored floral centerpieces. Wind ribbons in rich medieval colors of russet, hunter green, sky blue, and deep gold from the flowers to the edges of the table. Let tall white candles cast a warm glow over the entire table.

To make your reception truly medieval, set up the head table as if overlooking the royal subjects. Include roast pig, smoked salmon, stuffed dates, brie, and fresh berries in the royal menu.

Toasting should take place throughout the meal. Gift your attendants with pewter tankards imprinted with their names, great for authentic medieval toasts befitting a royal couple.

During the course of the dinner, a bugle should sound to announce a proclamation. (A tapping of flatware on glasses can take the place of the bugle.) then one of the medieval statues can read from a scroll, announcing a recision of taxes in honor of your royal marriage. When the announcement begins, two or three young members of the family, dressed as pages, hand out net bags of chocolate coins wrapped in gold foil. This continues until each guest is gifted with a favor of coins.

Of course, the gentle music of the mandolin and lute should be heard all through the day. Certainly the music, in addition to everything else, will have your guests singing the praises of this unique Camelot wedding.

ROMANTIC RENAISSANCE

What could be more romantic than this transitional time in Europe between the medieval and the modern? Back then, upper-class social gatherings were relaxed occasions in opulent and elegant surroundings. As a modern bride, you can take the best features of this classical period and apply them to selected parts of your wedding.

Garlands, wreaths, and swags of fruits, vegetables, leaves, and flowers tied together with ribbons were everywhere in this period. Imitate this look at your head table, cake table, and gift table with the modern version of the swag look. Run drapery roping in loops along the skirt length of the tables. Cluster fresh ivy strands at the top of each loop, letting the longer ivy strands drop down almost to the floor. Before you start arranging, condition the ivy by soaking the ivy (leaves and all) in cool water.

Think of your dining tables as a painting of the period. Center a compote (a shallow bowl with a base and stem) filled with clusters of purple, red, and green grapes on every table. Flank the compote with candelabras. Wind pink ribbon and ivy around the arms and base of the candelabra. Crystal candleholders can be substituted, but group the candles in assorted heights for extra visual interest.

This centerpiece should be set on a table covered with a white tablecloth and alternate pink, green, and lavender napkins. Add Renaissance-inspired favors to each place setting. Since fruit is often seen on tables in Renaissance paintings, assemble a basket of fruit. Arrange one perfect peach surrounded by small clusters of red and green grapes and ripe strawberries in a low, open basket. If you're feeling particularly generous, add a small decorative fruit knife to the basket, as well.

Apply the classic look to the cake, too. Order a layer cake with plastic pillers creating space between each layer. Decorate the space between each layer with fresh ivy, and use more ivy laced with pink ribbons around the base of the cake. Crown the cake with sugared grapes and ivy.

Venetian glass was also highly valued in this period. While you may not want to gift your attendants with expensive glass, you can select small glass paperweights as your thank-you to them and still be in keeping with your theme.

If desired, bring a touch of the Renaissance to your invitations. Find classically styled cards, or, if that isn't possible, have someone do a pen-and-ink drawing of a decorative swag. Make sure the printing used for the invitation is classic in appearance. Ask your stationer for advice.

Everything should be in keeping with this Renaissance mood . . . menu, music, dress, and gracious hosting. In other words, use the classic Renaissance look to turn your wedding into a *classy* affair!

VICTORIAN DELIGHT

This theme takes you back to a time of softness and beauty, a time when an extravagance of lace, ribbon, and flowers satisfied a passion for loveliness. This look, treasured and loved again, can create a wedding that will be a vision to behold.

You will be a vision to behold in a Victorian-style wedding dress. Shop for a dress that features a high neck, puff sleeves, and a tight-fitting waist. If bridal shop dresses aren't available in this style, look for dressmaker patterns. (See Historical Dress Pattern Sources, Fashion Guide, for mailing addresses of costume pattern companies.)

Original Victorian bouquets were secured with silver, ivory, or gold posey holders. With or without an antique posey holder, you can carry a lovely Victorian bouquet. Select a cluster bouquet of roses and incorporate old lace pieces either by fashioning the pieces into rosebuds (See Lace Rosebuds, Floral Guide) or letting the lace strips fall from the bouquet like ribbon streamers.

As for the attendants' gifts, give each bridesmaid a choker necklace to complement her dress. You can easily make these yourself. Select velvet ribbon about 3/4-inch wide, and secure a clasp on each end. Pin a broach or an old fancy button to the center of the ribbon, and you'll have an authentic Victorian jewelry piece. Give appropriate tie pins to the groom's attendants.

An easy way to achieve a Victorian look at the ceremony is to attach lace and ribbon bows with long streamers to the ends of the pews. At a later date, remembrance pillows for your bed or sofa can be made from the ribbon and lace.

Set a Victorian table for your guests. This is the time to bring out the linen tablecloths, pretty serving pieces, and paper lace liners. Add lavish floral centerpieces, and sprinkle flower petals on the tablecloth. Victorian table decorating doesn't stop at the table but brings the chairs into the picture, too. Tape lace bows and streamers or chair back bouquets of dried rosebuds, baby's breath, and statice to the backs of the chairs.

Complete the total look with one perfect rosebud favor at each place setting. Tie a bow of 1/8-inch picot ribbon around the rose, ending in long flowing strands. You can add a florist's stick pin for your guests' wearing convenience. Color-coordinate the rose and the ribbon to your table setting colors.

One final note. Keep friends and relatives busy at the reception with a little turn of the century boardwalk posing. Make a billboard with two holes cut large enough for heads. Paint a boardwalk and a bicycle-built-for-two scene around the cutouts. Then have a friend at the ready to snap pictures with a Polaroid camera. The fun is in the posing and the comparing of pictures later. Sometimes high schools have leftover billboards from proms or plays that you can use. As plans for your day unfold, keep adding old-fashioned Victorian touches to your new-fashioned wedding. This theme will add an aura of loveliness to your wedding that everyone will enjoy.

THE GREAT GATSBY

Do you lean toward the opulent, finding that too much isn't enough? This theme takes you back to those ultraextravagant days when food and garb were elegant and O-so-old-world European. Take a minute to close your eyes and see groups of beautiful people casually enjoying their luxurious surroundings. That's the scene you're going to recreate, for one day only, your wedding day.

Send formal invitations with old world script. Ask your printer to show you the available typesetting styles and pick the best, readable script that reminds you of the Gatsby period. In each invitation's envelope, add something to raise your guests' expectations . . . a pressed rose.

Wedding attire is next on the fantasy agenda. Groom and attendants wear black dinner jackets for evening, or black stroller, striped trousers, and gray waistcoats for daytime. Dresses should be reminiscent of the Gatsby time. Suggestion: Rent "The Great Gatsby" video to get a feel for the period. Or, lacking the video, ask your librarian for reference books that may have pictures of that era.

If you're really serious about creating this fantasy, you should consider renting a Great Gatsby—era estate, preferably one with a ballroom. The search for this kind of mansion will be easier if you contact your local historical society for names and places. Failing the estate, you may be able to find a restaurant whose design theme is from that period. Look for dark woods, red velvet, and elaborate chandeliers.

Still on the rental subject, it's a must that the wedding party have access to an old classic car. Certainly you, the wedding couple, should arrive at the reception in something like a stylish Packard convertible. Comb the newspapers for classic car rentals. Use the rental car as a backdrop for some classic Gatsby poses. Ask the photographer or a friend to be sure to get shots of everyone in the wedding party by the car. The snapshots will be the second part of your gift to your attendants. The first part of the gift will be Art Deco or Victorian-style frames given to your attendants at the rehearsal dinner or the day of your wedding.

Do the Gatsby look for eye-catching table settings. Use a black fabric tablecloth, red napkins with white china, and one perfect red rose in full bloom in a black vase. Black spray paint quickly converts an inexpensive glass vase to an expensive-looking one. If something like fringed silver filigree table lamps are available, use them, too.

Tuck the champagne bottles into decorative ice coolers. Put one empty container, the same circumference as a champagne bottle, into a large container. Pour distilled water around the sides and add a few flowers to the water. Roses freeze beautifully. Set the block of ice on a napkin-covered plate or foil-covered base on the tables (See Ice Coolers, Table Setting Guide.).

Favor each guest with one long stemmed chocolate rosebud. You'll find these at most candy boutiques. Present the roses in a silver basket or on a silver tray.

Good taste, or more correctly, *lots* of good taste, is the byword for this theme. Once everyone relaxes and allows the mood of their surroundings to sink in, they'll easily enjoy the fantasy this theme creates. Champagne, anyone?

FABULOUS FIFTIES

How's this for a not-so-long-ago theme? A pink and white color scheme, bouffant skirts, sunglasses, convertibles, and last, but not least, rock and roll! Ask anyone who was a young adult during the fifties for advice you can apply to your wedding day. Then prepare yourself for some fabulous fun and a whole new set of fifties memories.

Romance was *in* in the fifties, and bridal fashions were no exception. The perfect wedding dress featured a fitted bodice, an intriguing neckline, and a many-layered full, full skirt fit for a storybook princess. You may still find a pattern for a fifties-styled bridal gown, or better yet, you may be able to wear your mother''s wedding dress. The bridesmaids should be in pink dresses with bouffant skirts, and the men in the wedding party should wear white sport coats.

Bridal bouquets of the time were crescent-shaped or round, dainty, nosegays of white flowers. Bridesmaids should carry a smaller version of the bridal bouquet featuring pink and white carnations. Tuck a pink carnation with a spray of baby's breath into the men's lapels.

Of course, getting to and from ceremony to reception in the fifties mode means decorated cars . . . convertibles! Rent a classic fifties convertible from a car dealer specializing in that period, or settle for newer model convertibles and decorate them thoroughly. This should be a duty zealously performed by the attendants. Crêpe paper, cream, balloons, even old cans and shoes for tying to the bumper of the car are mandatory for decorating.

Once at the reception area, let your guests find themselves under a pink and white canopy of twisted paper streamers. Place centerpieces of pink and white carnations accented with baby's breath on the tables. Cover the tables with white tablecloths, and place pink personalized paper napkins at each setting.

You can add more of the fifties atmosphere to the table with a contemporary wedding feature . . . favors for the wedding guest. Purchase small plastic toy convertibles, and fill them with individually wrapped candies. Secure the candy to the car with a strip of pink netting long enough to wrap around the midsection of the car and candy, and tie in a large bow. Set these favors at each place setting.

For your activity-minded guests, plan a genuine fifties record hop with a disc jockey for after-dinner entertainment. Open the dancing with the all-time rock and roll favorite "Rock Around the Clock." Follow this up with your theme's song, "A White Sport Coat and a Pink Carnation." by this time everyone will be ready to dance to other oldies like the "Bunny Hop" and "the Stroll." Yet another way to emphasize the fifties is to give a theme gift to the attendants. Choose from either of these ideas. Engrave identification bracelets, popular in the fifties, with the name of your attendant. Or, buy fun, casual wristwatches for the attendants and enclose a note saying, "Thank you for helping us rock around the clock while celebrating our marriage."

Whether or not your guests ever wore fifties sunglasses or drank cherry colas, they'll still relate to the style and enthusiasm of this theme. So get set. It's time to rock around the clock!

6. Holiday Themes

S hould your wedding date fall near a major holiday, you'll have the added gaity of the holiday to encourage everyone into a celebrating frame of mind. Not only that, but you'll have a wealth of holiday ideas and materials at your disposal to help you plan a smashing wedding.

HEARTS & FLOWERS

What holiday can better demonstrate love and romance than Valentines Day? This sentimental hearts-and-flowers celebration is filled to the brim with romantic overtones. You'll have no trouble finding trimmings and decorations for this, your love—ly wedding day.

Let yourself go and immerse yourself in this romantic world. Fill your reception space with red, white, and pink crèpe paper streamers, white paper wedding bells, silver heart-shaped balloons, red foil hearts, and pink and white bows . . . bows . . . bows everywhere!

Carry this romantic theme to the dining tables, too. Feature red floral centerpieces on white tablecloths. Stand pink and white candles on either side of the flowers and scatter little red hearts on the tablecloth around both flowers and candles. Tuck a Valentine lollipop favor into a pink, folded napkin, and tie together with a strip of netting.

Add to the traditional wedding day activities with touches of Valentine symbols. For instance, substitute tiny red foil hearts for rice, and wrap in white and pink netting. Throwing rice or, in this case, confetti, on the bride and groom signifies a life of plenty for the new-lyweds. Put the packets of confetti in net-lined, white wicker baskets to be passed out by the younger members of the wedding party.

Continue the romantic symbolism in the wedding cake. Select a heart-shaped cake decorated with pink hearts made of icing. Two Cupids perched on top of the cake complete this romantic confection. Add a circle of netting to the base of the cake tray.

At each side of the cake, place white wicker trays of freshly baked cookie favors. Order Cupid-shaped cookies from the bakery, and either you or the bakery can decorate the Cupids with tiny pink frost-ed hearts. Finish off with gold string tied around the Cupids' necks. (See Cupid Cookies, Decorative Recipe Guide, for how to decorate.)

Punch up the refreshment table with servings of Love Potion Number Nine Punch. This pink punch is tasty as well as decorative. (See Love Potion Number Nine, Decorative Recipe Guide.) Keep the punch chilled with floating heart-shaped ice cubes, and prop a lace-trimmed card scripted with the recipe's name against the punch bowl.

Music, too, lends itself to this romance-inspire theme. Turn that first wedding dance into a musical moment to remember. Dance to the all-time favorite, "My Funny Valentine." Include special-to-you love songs to be played through the night. To be safe, request the selections well ahead of the wedding date so the band has time to prepare.

Invite your wedding guests to this major event with heart-inspired invitations. If you're from the casual but unique school of thought, print the invitations in red ink on pink paper. Slip a sprinkling of tiny red hearts into the invitations before sealing. Brighten the invitation by sealing the envelope flap with a red foil heart.

As you attend to each detail of your wedding, more heart and flower ideas will come to you. As an example, you might choose a heart-shaped ring pillow, favor your guests with small velvet and lace hearts filled with potpourri, or gift your attendants with fountain pens and a bottle of red ink.

Use all or any of these theme ideas and you can be sure your guests will respond with heartfelt enthusiasm.

EASTER CELEBRATION

This time of year signals new beginnings, as the Easter holiday demonstrates so well. This theme, then, will put all the joy and optimism of the holiday into your wedding. See how your wedding can be beautifully enhanced with the addition of selected Easter symbols.

Limit the decorations at the ceremony itself to Easter lilies and ribbon. Tape one Easter lily to each pew trimmed with a generous length of satin ribbon. (See Attaching Pew Markers, Decorations for the Ceremony.) Set one or two pots of lilies decorated with satin bows and streamers in the sanctuary.

Because lilies are used for the church decorations, they should be one of the featured flowers in the bouquets, too. Decide on a striking bridal bouquet of white lilies and freesia. The bridesmaids will make their own Easter statement carrying straw baskets filled to overflowing with pastel lilies, freesia, tulips, and heather. Natural straw baskets can be spray-painted white or a pastel wedding color. Use the same kind of straw baskets for the centerpieces as well. Spray-paint them to match the tabletop colors, and fill with Easter grass and all sizes of honeycomb paper eggs. Attach a big bow to the handle and tie extra ribbon streamers around the handle so a cascade of ribbon comes down and around the basket.

Multicolored jelly beans poured into plastic champagne glasses make colorful favors. Pastel-coated, round, chocolate candies can be used instead and are available at this time of year. Press plastic cling wrap to the top and sides of the glass so the candy will stay in place. Punch a straw through the wrap and down into the candy. Before putting everything together, paste paper strips, large enough to print your names and the date of your wedding, to the straws. Complete the project by tying several strands of curly ribbon to the stems of the champagne glasses to give them party favor status.

The Easter bunny shares center stage, too. Set two plush bunnies dressed as bride and groom on the guest book or cake table. For sheer whimsical fun, rent a plush, life-size rabbit and set it prominently at the reception entrance to greet the guests. Hang an Easter basket filled with net bags of birdseed. If you have the time, spray-paint inexpensive plastic eggs and fill them with birdseed.

This theme is easy to work with because many of these decorative suggestions are already on hand or can easily be found. With a little borrowing from the Easter holiday, your wedding will be remembered by all as an eggs—tra special day!

FLAG-WAVING FESTIVAL

Set off this theme with a veritable explosion of red, white, and blue. Patriotic fervor and romantic fever combine forces here to create a gala celebration. Simply borrow the decor from the Fourth of July and get set for a flag-waving good time. Stars and stripes forever and . . . everywhere!

Color your bouquets in patriotic red, white, and blue. Select large or small red carnations (carnations give a true red color), white sparkle pompons (their shape is reminiscent of fireworks), and blue flowers (either blue, stem-dyed daisies or bachelor buttons). And finally, tie a red, white, and blue striped bow to finish off the bouquet with a flourish.

Use the same striped ribbon liberally at your church or temple. Tie large striped bows around the candles, flowerpots, and ends of pews.

Bridesmaid dresses can follow a blue and white color scheme, perhaps in a nautical style. Straw hats get the nod as head toppers, complementing the nautical-style dresses.

Several possibilities suggest themselves when considering how the invitations can reflect your theme. A favorite includes tucking a paper miniature flag or tiny red stars into each invitation. Then place the invitation into white envelopes lined with red or blue and seal the flaps with red or blue stars.

As your guests enter the reception area, greet them with the strains of "Yankee Doodle Dandy" and these eyecatching patriotic center-pieces . . . fanciful rockets alongside red, white, and blue flowers. (See Patriotic Centerpiece, Centerpiece Guide, for how-to directions.)

Fill out the centerpiece with onion grass. Onion grass is sometimes called silver exploding paper because tiny strips of foil seem to explode off the stems. You can curl the foil strips by running your fingers down the edges. Onion grass is available at craft or flower shops.

Since fireworks as well as rockets are an expected part of a Fourth of July celebration, try a firecracker napkin holder arrangement. Cardboard tubes, a little paint, curling ribbon, and napkins are all you need. (See Firecracker Napkin Ring Arrangement, Table Setting Guide, for instructions.)

For entertainment, what else? Present a fireworks show timed for the first minutes of darkness. At the same time, favor your guests with small packages of sparklers, wrapped with red, blue, and white striped ribbon. Let everyone share the celebration spirit.

This theme will be a gala reminder of a great country's beginnings, as well as your celebration of a great beginning as a couple.

GIVING THANKS

This is one theme you can't overdo. Thanksgiving is a time of bounty, full of the warmth of family gatherings, the abundance of food, and a blaze of color. You'll be proud to invite your family and friends to this bountiful, harvest home, wedding celebration.

Whenever possible, draw color inspiration for dress or table from munificent nature at harvesttime. For example, bridesmaids' dresses can be made in the rich colors of autumn leaves, russet apples, or bittersweet berries. You'll find the perfect contrasting color in the blue of the autumn sky.

Chrysanthemums are a tried and true bouquet choice for fall weddings. Dried flower bouquets are another popular alternative. Or, join the trend towards looser bouquets. This kind of bouquet is simply a bunch of flowers, stems intact, tied loosely together. For this theme, a loose bouquet of gerbera daisies could be used. Whatever the choice, flowers should reflect the style of wedding, whether formal or casual.

Dress your dining tables in autumn gold cloths toped with wisps of lace pieces here and there. Drape candleholders with lace, tie lace pieces around the napkins in loose knots, and add lace bows to the stems of goblets.

At each table, center a horn of plenty spilling with the abundance of a harvest garden. Your banquet facilities may already have the cornucopias for the fall season. If not, you can easily find reed or wicker cornucopias in craft shops. Fill the cornucopias with clean dry fruits and vegetables of the season. (Enjoy a shopping spree at the local farmers market.) Complete the setting with candles at each side.

This theme deserves a favor good for a gobble or two. Set a small lifelike turkey candle at each place setting and prop a personalized matchbook against the base. You can order the matchbooks with your imprinted names at the same place and time as you order your invitations.

The menu for this time of year deserves special consideration. *Don't* repeat the traditional turkey and trimmings. Instead, serve some kind of game such as venison. It will express the spirit of the holiday theme without forcing your guests to eat two large turkey dinners within a short time.

How to entertain within the framework of the holiday? Enlist the help of the local high school or college drama group. With their help, write a short humorous script detailing the pilgrim love story of John Alden and Priscilla Mullens. But instead of following the story line religiously, upgrade the story with personal and funny stories of your courtship days. *Silly* and *fun* are the operative words here. Treat this drama as after-dinner entertainment, or schedule it during the dance band's break.

Give thanks to your attendants with a harvest sampler of nuts, fruits, and foil-wrapped candies. Ask a gift shop to arrange the treats decoratively in a wicker cornucopia or basket, and shrink-wrap them. The goodies will taste good in the days following the festivities, and the wicker container will hold any number of household items, a pretty and practical reminder of your wedding day.

Consider these theme ideas as pieces of a puzzle designed to enhance your wedding. Once the day arrives, you will relax and enjoy the total picture in good spirits.

MISTLETOE & POINSETTIA

It's true! You can't celebrate too much over the holidays. So planning a wedding around Yuletide festivities just adds to the wedding merriment. This theme relies on the fact that seasonal flowers and decorations will most likely be in place at the church and reception.

Though poinsettias and seasonal decorations will be in place, Christmas-ise your wedding ceremony even more by taping large red bows with long hanging ribbons (gypsies use red for good luck) to each pew. Tack tiny silver bells to the ends of each ribbon. The faint sounds of jingling bells will be heard depending on the whim of the air current.

Additional seasonal sound effects will be heard if you attach tiny bells to the bouquets. They'll jingle with every movement. A warm alternative to floral bouquets are furry hand muffs decorated with one blossom and bells.

As the song says, deck the halls with an abundance of Christmas decorations. Mistletoe, a romantic holiday symbol, couldn't be more appropriate at a wedding reception. To the druids of ancient England, a kiss under the "magick plant" meant a promise of marriage. Hang mistletoe with white bows in busy areas, any place where the crowd will walk through or linger for a while. Mistletoe encourages plenty of high jinks, just the thing for camera or video pictures.

Another holiday tradition to work into your wedding day is the holiday fruitcake. If it's customary in your area to have a groom's cake, select fruitcake. Have the caterer or Santa's elves cut the groom's cake into small pieces and wrap in small white boxes tied with holiday-colored ribbon or string. Set the boxes on the same table as the wedding cake.

Fill in an empty spot in the reception area with a favor-decorated Christmas tree. Trim the tree with glass ball ornaments imprinted with your names and wedding date. You'll have a pretty tree, and the favors will be easily accessible to your guests. Miniatures of an interest or hobby shared by you and your groom are good alternatives to the glass balls. While shopping for the favors, you might as well find interesting tree trimmings to say thank you to your wedding attendants.

Still into the Christmas spirit, gift wrap the reception tables as if they were large Christmas gifts. Cover with white tablecloths and stretch 3-inch-wide ribbon end to end, as if you were wrapping the top half of a gift box. Complete the gift box look with a big bow in the center. Arrange shiny glass ball ornaments in and about the bow, and sprinkle glitter on everything. Set candles close by so that the glass balls and glitter reflect the candle flame, doubling the reflection value. Finish off with gold metallic gift cards at each place setting to serve as place cards.

Entertainment is easy. Simply arrange for a harpist and flutist to play yuletide tunes or invite costumed Merry England carolers to serenade your guests for their dining enjoyment. Reserve your group early. This advice is equally important for any of your wedding arrangements. Bookings are usually made at least a year in advance in most areas for dates at this time of year.

Since more of your relatives and friends will be at home to enjoy the holidays, it makes sense to celebrate your wedding at this time when more people can attend. You'll agree, this theme combines the two best reasons for celebration . . . Christmas and the start of a new life together. A clink of the eggnog cup, then, for a truly joyous wedding and Noel!

7. Heritage Themes

P sst . . . your heritage is showing! What better time to display pride in one's heritage then when celebrating a wedding. These themes give you a variety of meaningful and decorative ways to highlight your cultural background.

ETHNIC DRESS

The focus of this theme is on the dress of the wedding party as well as flowers and headwear. Dress and accessories give you an opportunity to highlight each of your ethnic backgrounds in a way that is personally meaningful to you. Since all cultural backgrounds can't possibly be covered, try to read those ideas you particularly enjoy as if they applied to your heritage.

The bride who wishes to emphasize her heritage may consider wearing an authentic bridal dress of her heritage. Other brides may simply choose to underline their heritage by choosing symbolic accessories. For example, the English bride could slip a sixpence into her shoe, or the Chinese bride might wear a jade pendant.

If desired, brides can exchange their wedding dress for an authentic folk dress after the ceremony. The Slovak bride exchanges the white bridal veil for a kerchief after the ceremony to signify the rite of passage to the married state.

Since the groom may not be of the same cultural background as the bride, he should also dress in a way that displays his heritage. If he is

Scottish, he might wear a kilt. Then again, if he is Irish, he could simply wear a four-leaf clover in his lapel; if of German descent, a sprig of edelweiss. Stoles or sashes representative of one's heritage can also be worn.

Color can play a cultural role, too. For example, red is recognized by some cultures as denoting happiness and joy. Other cultures wear red for good luck. If all else fails, represent your heritage simply by the choice of colors you wear.

Child attendants can have the honor of representing your culture. Dress them in ethnic costumes to highlight your heritage.

Headpieces are often an important factor in wedding customs. A beautiful, elaborate wedding crown is worn by the Swedish bride. Here in America, these bridal crowns are often rented from local Swedish cultural organizations. Stefan crowns—narrow, white bands worn by bride and bridegroom and connected by one satin ribbon—are a part of the Greek Orthodox wedding. The linked crowns signify a commitment to one life together.

Another accessory easily transformed into a symbolic statement is the bouquet. Blossoms can be chosen for the colors that represent the cultures. Certain symbolic additions to the bridal bouquet will accentuate your heritage. Wheat, a Scandinavian symbol of fertility, could be added to the bouquet. A simpler approach to honoring one's heritage is to choose a flower native to one's culture, for the bouquet. As you can see, a little thought in choosing wedding attire and flowers can highlight your ethnic heritage in a becoming fashion. Colors and costumes of your culture can do much to display pride in your heritage.

ETHNIC CEREMONY

This theme shows how any symbols of your culture added to the ceremony, whether in music, readings, or exchanging of vows, can display your pride in the past and your creative hope for the future. Select any of the following ideas to make your ceremony uniquely personal.

Music is always enjoyable, especially when a soft medley of ethnic tunes is played before the ceremony. During the ceremony, an ethnic song could be performed by a vocalist or instrumentalist. Yet another way is to incorporate ethnic music into the recessional wedding march. For instance, bagpipes or the rhythmic beat of drums can accompany the march. Look for ethnic music in the music department of your library, music societies, or local cultural organizations.

Perhaps an ethnic flavor could be adapted to the readings. For example, love poems written by poets of your heritage can be read aloud. Then again, an expression of philosophy stemming from your heritage can be shared with your guests. Perhaps a short exchange of love and devotion to each other expressed out loud in the language of your heritage would give just the right note to your ceremony.

The rituals surrounding your exchanging of vows are important, too. In Japan, for instance, couples take ceremonious sips of sake (rice wine). The sharing of wine is part of the Jewish ceremony as well as of the Greek and other Eastern Orthodox churches.

The place a couple exchanges wedding vows can be just as interesting as what they do while exchanging vows. For example, the Jewish couple exchanges vows under a huppah(an ornamental canopy symbolizing shelter). Any ritual like that represents your heritage and can be a part of your ceremony.

Think about liturgical dancing (dancing during a religious ceremony) as a possible idea to include into your ceremony. A dance performed to the strains of a ballad or folk song from your heritage would be a fitting highlight to your ceremony. After the ceremony, the performing dancer could lead the guests out of the church with a simple folk dance.

Strictly speaking, invitations aren't part of the ceremony. But they are an expression of your intent to marry. Delight your guests with invitations written in English and the language of your heritage. In some cases, you might use English and two or more different languages.

Any of these ideas, of course, should be discussed with your priest, minister, or rabbi. Once you have the go-ahead, plunge into the planning with gusto.

Find more ideas by talking to your grandparents about their wedding, researching your culture, and putting the gray matter in your head to work. The result of all this will be a ceremony not to be duplicated, a ceremony personally yours.

ETHNIC FOOD AND TABLE SETTING

Here is a taste-filled theme. Authentic recipes, linens, and serving pieces will help you highlight your heritage. Rely on the timeless tradition of serving food and drink to make your celebration a cultural success.

Prepare your own food or arrange to have a caterer prepare a special menu featuring foods from your heritage. In Kenya, relatives, friends, and neighbors donate and prepare the wedding food, a tradition in itself. The Scandinavian Smorrebrod (always a variety of open-faced sandwiches) offers a good example of a great spread. Then again, an Italian menu might consist of an aperitif of white wine, fresh fruit chilled with Marsala, and plenty of pasta. Restaurants of your ethnic persuasion and festival-of-nation cookbooks are a good starting point to plan a complete ethnic menu or just a few dishes.

A sampling of dishes from your heritage is especially appealing in unions of two or more cultures. Feature one food group, such as breads, to showcase your heritage. Selections like Kolacky, a sweet bun topped with poppy seeds, representing the Eastern European heritage, scones with clotted cream and strawberry preserves from England, and a Ukranian wedding bread, Korovai, decorated with symbolic motifs representing eternity and union of two families all tastefully highlight a heritage.

Table settings can also reflect your heritage. Draping the head table with an embroidered ethnic tablecloth is a beautiful way to display your heritage. Inscribing the champagne toasting glasses in the language of your choice is a good way to toast each other as well as your heritage. Or, use a few select serving pieces in the colors or design of your heritage to tell your story.

Of course, centerpieces readily complete the tabletop heritage theme. Combine flowers with English teapots, porcelain dragons, Russian samovars, pinatas, Lladro or Hummel figurines, or leprechauns. Or how about using miniature national flags as individual centerpieces? This kind of centerpiece can unify your theme visually and decoratively.

Favors for your table add to the heritage flavor, too. Set small calendars printed in your ethnic language by each place setting. Circle the wedding date on the calendar in red. Wrap traditional candies from your culture with paper and ribbon in the color representing your heritage. Or, simply box up a special ethnic treat. If an ethnic dish is especially popular, print the recipe on decorative note cards and set one at each place setting.

Inspiration is everywhere . . . ethnic festivals, family hand-me-down treasures and recipes, and travel and history sections of libraries. A little research will give you the confidence to share your heritage.

ETHNIC WEDDING CUSTOMS

This theme injects an ethnic note into reception activities, bringing charm and joy to the wedding day. It's a nice way to go back in time and celebrate your link with the past. It's also an opportunity for friends and family to enjoy the ethnic fun and activities your culture has to offer.

Toasting, a time-honored tradition in itself, provides an opportunity to honor the union with an ethnic salute. By all means, serve a beverage unique to your heritage, such as Scandinavian aquavit, German lager, French wine, Spanish champagne, or Portuguese madeira. And whether it's "Prosit!" "Skol!" "Salud!" or "Cheers!" it all means the same . . . sincere good wishes.

Let the wedding cake represent your heritage, as well as giving your guests an unexpected taste treat. Here are some possible cake selections in all their heritage splendor. Picture yourself cutting into an Austrian *Sacher Torte*, a chocolate cake served with whipped cream, a French *Choux à la Creme*, a pyramid of small puff pastries filled with cream, or a Scandinavian, *Kronsekage*, flat round ring cakes of different sizes stacked to form a pyramid.

If you select a traditional white cake, then a cake topper can represent your culture. Consider creating handmade, ethnic costumed figures as a cake topper representing you and your groom. Symbols of your heritage are another possibility. For example, heather represents Scotland; good luck dragons, Eastern lands; a tiny cuckoo clock, Austria; or a Venetian glass piece, Italy.

A simple secret to ensure a joyous wedding celebration is ethnic music. Ethnic music created by drums, bagpipes, accordions, harp, lute, guitar, or castanets guarantees your guests' listening enjoyment. When live performers can't be found, use taped music.

During the band's intermission, engage ethnic performers to put on a folk dance show. Ethnic dance clubs or a children's dance class are good sources. They'll give a colorfully costumed performance. Anything goes here. So seriously consider hiring a professional Scottish sword dance ensemble, a spirited flamenco dancer, or a Chinese lion dance team to ward off bad luck and evil spirits.

Better yet, have the band lead the guests through folk dances like the polka, horah, Greek handkerchief dance, Italian tarantella, Irish jig, or Scottish Highland fling. Encourage the guests who know the dance steps to put on a how-to demonstration. You'll have exhausted but happy guests on your hands once the band stops playing.

The extra thought given to this kind of wedding will generate dividends of good cheer. Its activities will bring everyone to appreciate and enjoy your culture as they join in the celebration of your marriage.

Destination
8. Themes

U se a glamorous honeymoon destination as the theme inspiration for your wedding day. The same sparkle, excitement, and fun that you anticipate for your honeymoon can help you plan a vacationlike setting for your wedding.

HAWAIIAN LUAU

You can't take your guests with you, but you can treat them to a colorful luau. Create an island of tranquility with a luxuriant profusion of greenery, flowers, leis, island music, and food with a Hawaiian flavor.

Greet each guest with a traditional Hawaiian lei as their personal favor. Fresh flower leis are beautiful, but inexpensive paper leis can offer a touch of color and festivity, too. Flowers most often strung in Hawaiian leis are the plumeria, carnation, and orchid. Other flowers more accessible on the mainland can be used for successful lei making. Try asters, daisies, cornflowers, and marigolds.

Remember, a certain tradition must be observed when presenting a lei. A hug or kiss is always given as the lei is placed over the shoulders. The lei should be worn in a graceful drape over the shoulders, with a little of the lei hanging down the back.

Carry the tropical flower theme to any wedding bouquets, too. Select beautiful tropical flowers like sweet-scented orchids, plumeria, or tuberose. One sprig or blossom of any of these flowers can serve as a lapel flower, as well.

Decorate your reception area with arrangements of anthuriums, bird of paradise, hibiscus, and canna leaves, or any large, glossy leaves. Set torches alongside paths leading to the reception area, or set torches outside in dramatic arrangements in front of windows for the guests' viewing enjoyment.

Enjoy food with a Hawaiian flavor as another addition to this tropical setting. Serve a menu that includes plenty of pineapples, guavas, avocados, bananas, coconuts, and macadamia nuts. And, no luau is complete without the roasted pig.

Satisfying tropical refreshments such as mai tais, piña coladas, and so on, with or without the alcohol, serve as decorative elements as well as refreshments, if served in coconut halves and a tropical bloom is placed on top along with a ring of pineapple.

Tuck ferns and flowers among the serving dishes. Place large green leaves under the serving dishes. Do the same for the base of the wedding cake. Then, top the wedding cake with more tropical flowers. Effort should be made to give an abundant, lush, tropical look to everything.

Of course, dinner music should include well-known Hawaiian songs, and the "Hawaiian Wedding Song" should lead off the dancing. During the band''s break, a hula dance lesson can entertain everyone. Get someone to start and then encourage the others to join in this traditional dance.

This tropical experience can be transplanted to any locale at any time of the year. You can be sure a good time will be shared by all . . . right down to the last gentle *aloha*!

OLD MEXICO

For sheer color and flash you can't top this theme, solely inspired by our neighbor to the south. Your guests will get caught up in all the gaity and spontaneity that Old Mexico has to offer. For you, it will be an exciting prelude to your honeymoon destination.

Picture the bridal party dresses dazzling in white summer cotton, with the bride's dress topped by a white lace sash and the bridesmaids' dresses accented with brightly colored sashes and matching shoes. The same colors used for the sashes should be used for the groom's and attendants' cummerbunds. Each bridesmaid should carry a striking bouquet of strawflowers, daisies, zinnias, and bee balm in assorted hot-salsa colors and garnished with striped grosgrain ribbons.

The reception area should match the festive dress of your wedding party. Spread white linen tablecloths on the tables and top with one or more casually draped serapes (small, brightly colored blankets). Place a wide-brimmed sombrero in the center of the table. Put two or three roly poly lights within the brim of the hat and spread strawflower blossoms around and about the candles. Complete the table setting with a variety of hot-colored napkins, plaid or plain.

In this case, the menu adds to the decorative flavor already dictated by the table linen and centerpieces. Indulge your guests with an American-Mexican menu of tacos, burritos, chimichangas, refried beans, Spanish rice and, for dessert, caramel-topped flan. Set individual dishes of flan around the wedding cake.

If possible, hire strolling musicians in costumes to strum soft romantic Mexican songs or perhaps select tapes of Mexican music to be played before and during dinner. After-dinner dancing can include lessons in Mexican folk dancing and selected dance music. Work closely with your band so you know what is possible.

Schedule the time-honored tradition of pinata breaking during the band's breaks. Pinatas are fanciful figures made of papier mâché. Hollow inside, they are traditionally stuffed with candies and trinkets. One person is blindfolded and handed a stout stick with which to break the hanging pinata. When the pinata is broken, everyone scrambles for the falling treats. Everyone, young or old, can participate.

Fill the pinata with trinkets or mementos marking this special day. Bear in mind that the mementos must be small enough to fit into the pinata and nonbreakable when they fall to the floor. Small gourds, combs imprinted with your wedding date, and miniature bride and groom dolls are some suggestions. It's best to scour the import shops well before the wedding.

Gift your personal attendants with treasures from Mexico, as well. Silver, engraved Mexican combs, pocket-sized for the men, mantilla-sized for the women, will be appreciated.

Fill in any empty reception corners with baskets of large paper flowers and pinatas, all shapes and sizes. Both flowers and pinatas are easily found in import shops, or you can make them yourself. Find how-to directions in craft stores.

This theme will surround you with warmth . . . of hot colors, spicy food, and warm wishes. Everyone will be sure to shout a loud *Olé!* for this special day.

NEW YORK, NEW YORK!

This theme is all about the thrill and excitement of New York's Broadway. Definitely nighttime doings, decorations and activities will revolve around show biz. So confirm a date for a large hall and let's get on with the show!

Your first task is to transform a large hall into Broadway. Begin by renting a billboard, much like a theater marquee, that will light up your names, giving you top billing. Then aim for a Broadway flash of light throughout the evening.

Do this with several spotlights highlighting special activities . . . your first dance together, cutting the wedding cake, throwing the bridal bouquet, and so on.

Strings of white lights strung about will add more Broadway atmosphere. So will old and new, colorful Broadway show posters tacked to the walls and support columns.

Table centerpieces also demand a certain theater sophistication. Talk it over with your florist and together aim for all-white bouquets. Elevate them for dramatic effect. Use plastic pillars (any florist will know what you're talking about) for height, and set white candles in clear roly-polys underneath the flower arrangement. White dendrobiums give a sweeping spray look, while a few white roses and freesia tucked in exude a subtle fragrance. For greenery, add isolepsis, a pearlized grass.

For the bridal bouquet, choose an all-white bouquet of calla lilies and the same dendrobiums, roses, and freesias as used in the centerpieces. Omit the calla lilies but keep the white dendrobiums, roses, and freesias for a sophisticated look for the bridesmaids' bouquets.

More Broadway embellishments could be New York cheese cake added to the menu as an alternative dessert selection. Another treat is this favor idea: Bag a bagel for your guests for their morning after. Use glossy paper, lunch-size sacks that can be found in gift, stationery, or partyware shops, Any Broadway patron or wedding guest will relish the pleasure of waking up the next morning to a breakfast of bagels and cream cheese. Give one breakfast favor to each guest.

Solve attendant gifting quickly by purchasing tapes or CDs of the latest Broadway musicals. Gift wrap using paper printed with musical notes, or draw a black musical staff and notes on white paper.

Which brings us to hiring an orchestra or big band for your dining and dancing enjoyment. Look over their program before hiring them and make sure they will play plenty of Broadway show tunes. At intermission time arrange to have a dance line strut their stuff for more show time entertainment. Inquire about dance lines at the local college or high school.

There you have it. If it's a dramatic and exciting wedding celebration you're after, you can be sure this theme will play its part to your satisfaction.

KEY LARGO

Whether Florida and the Lower Keys are a dream destination or a honeymoon reality, turn your celebration into a salute to this romantic getaway. Strictly meant to be fun, this theme emphasizes sandy beaches, pink flamingos, and romantic Key Largo.

Seashells are often a treasured reminder of days spent on the beach. Either use the shells from your collection or find new ones to create a unique bouquet. Ask your florist to use seashells as the focal point of a cascade style bouquet. Then, fill in with any favorite seasonal flowers. An example might be a selection of pompons, candy tuft, lilies, and sweetheart roses. Order similar but smaller bouquets for the bridesmaids.

The table settings can easily be arranged to catch the imagination of your guests. Caribbean blue tablecloths or, at the least, white tablecloths with Caribbean blue napkins are the perfect color foil for the pink flamingos. Glue 4-to 6-inch-high feathered flamingos to scallop seashells. (You'll recognize the scallop shell as the logo for a major oil company.) Your florist can order the flamingos from Sullivan and Silk, a wholesale supplier. You or a friend, adept at calligraphy, can then personalize the favors by writing names and the date of your wedding on the shell. Use a fine-point, felt-tip, calligraphy pen.

Complete the table setting by planning a centerpiece of seashells, a few flowers, and a flamingo the same size as was used for the favors. Stand the flamingo in a saucer filled with a thin layer of sand. Arrange a few flowers, forming a high vertical line, alongside the flamingo and scatter small shells about the base of the arrangement.

Make the cake table seaworthy, as well. Drape swags of smilax around the table, fixing clusters of flowers and seashells at each high point of the swag. Crown the table with a key lime cake or a white cake with key lime filling, accented with twists of fresh lime and flowers.

It's always a good idea to select attendant gifts to fit in with the spirit of the theme you are using. In this case, popular inflatable drink holders are fun as well as easy to obtain, especially during the pool season. Flamingo-imprinted T-shirts are another option. Either of these fun-in-the-sun gifts will provide lasting, fond memories of your wedding day.

Finally, flash the 1948 Key Largo movie on a large screen. This Humphrey Bogart movie, if it's silent playing, can be run continuously in the same reception area. Mature guests will enjoy seeing their favorite actors again, and the younger set will enjoy the ageless romance theme. It's certain to promote conversation among your guests.

Guests always enjoy theme-inspired touches. Even a small detail like a rendition of "Moon Over Miami" played by the band will be appreciated. But whether you add more or less of these theme ideas to your celebration, your guests will be sure to appreciate their time spent in this romantic fantasy haven.

JAMAICA BOUND

Enjoy a preview of things to come with this tropical theme. Tasty food, rhythmic music, and exotic flowers can turn a so-so reception into a Caribbean vacation. Though Jamaica may be a distant destination, you can provide everything for your wedding just as if you were there.

Think tropical and plan a lush background for your proceedings. Rent hibiscus trees, usually available from February through the summer and set in strategic spots. Bank potted ferns and bougainvillea around the trees. Use palm fronds and tiki torches for added interest. Tiki torches come in tall and short sizes. The short, 2-foot torches are good for lining pathways. You'll need torch fuel, too, so pick that up at the same place you find the torches.

Exotic flowers are a must for bouquets as well as centerpieces for the dinner tables. Choose from orange, pink, and red hibiscus, purple or hot pink bougainvillea, and tropical orchids. The florist can arrange the flowers of your choice in a loose, casual bouquet, perfect for this relaxing tropical theme.

As for the centerpiece, simply place a few hibiscus blossoms around a clear bubble bowl of floating candles. The diameter of the bowl should be wide enough to allow the heat from the candle flame to escape, about 8 to 10 inches. You'll find these bowls at most import or inexpensive glass shops.

Line the buffet tables with mounds of fresh fruit. Serve barbecue chicken, Jamaican style. (It's the kind of hot food you eat when you are prepared to pay the price.) Your caterer should be able to find an authentic Jamaican Chicken recipe in a Jamaican cookbook. Cool the heat off with cold beverages, including Red Stripe, a Jamaican beer, Certainly offer another main dish for the less adventuresome.

Rather than the traditional, tiered, white wedding cake, substitute pineapple upside-down cake. Offer alternative tropical desserts like kiwi pie and banana cake.

Dine and dance to the beat of a reggae band. The rhythmic beat is bound to start feet tapping. Or, dance to the beat of steel drums. Any authentic island music will relax and beguile your guests. Taped music is an easy alternative to live music.

Sometimes, attendants' gifts pose last-minute planning problems. For this theme, gold-or silver-plated sand dollar charms can be a simple and "charming" solution. The bridesmaids can attach the sand dollars to a charm bracelet and the male attendants can put theirs on a gold chain.

Although favors may not be as imperative as attendant gifts for a wedding, they do present a wonderful caring thoughtfulness to your guests. With this in mind, place pretty fresh hibiscus hairpins or lapel flowers, as the case may be, next to each place setting. This simple touch of the tropics will add so much,

The point of this theme is to provide a tropical rest and relaxation time for everyone attending your wedding. That means you, too. So make your arrangements well ahead of time and then sit back and enjoy a relaxing, stress-free day.

9. Seasonal Themes

E ach theme is planned to help you make the most of a season. Whether winter or summer, spring or fall, you will be able to create the kind of wedding enjoyed and pleasantly remembered by all.

SPRING IS HERE

Here is a way to capture lightheartedness and gaity for your wedding, a way to put spring into your wedding preparations and shake off the winter doldrums. Some people get giddy at the slightest hint of spring so there's no telling what will happen when your guests are treated to this spring-filled theme.

Although you may be making decisions on a cold winter's day, keep thinking pastel colors and spring flowers. Daisies, wonderful daisies, should come to mind. Even the smallest detail of a wedding benefits from the addition of this lovely spring flower. Daisies are always available and reasonable in cost, too.

Select a nosegay of white daisies and ivy for the bridal bouquet and have daisies color matched for the maid's bouquets. Daisies are easy to work with because they offer a wide range of color choices. If you can't find the right color, bring a swatch of fabric to the florist and the daisies can be stem dyed to match. The pompon daisy holds up best throughout the day.

Add a backing of cluny lace to the daisy nosegay. Cluny comes in white or ivory, in a 6-, 8-, or 10-inch round backing. It can be spray-painted a matching color.

Now, how about some daisies for the flower girl? Fill a straw basket with stemmed daisies, and ask your flower girl to hand out daisies as she walks down the aisle. Tell the little one to walk in a zigzag pattern so that she gives equal time to both sides. Set aside an extra basket of daisies . . . reserved for those guests who missed a daisy at the ceremony.

Since you're aiming for a fresh springtime look, ask permission to hang a personalized windsock in place of a banner near the altar. Children's pinwheels add to this happy, carefree look, too. Simply tuck a pinwheel through the knot of each ribbon-and-bow pew marker. The air movement will turn the pinwheels. Add pots of daisies for your floral accents.

Pretty daisy centerpieces can be made for the reception dining tables with the help of fireside baskets. These are open-ended, oval base baskets with handles. Add a child's sprinkling can, a bouquet of daisies, and miniature garden tools to the arrangement. (See Fireside Basket Centerpiece, in the Centerpiece Guide, for detailed instructions.)

Packets of garden seeds placed casually on the basket centerpiece can double as favors for your guests. Add enough seed packets so that each person sitting at the table gets a favor. Choose seeds that are common to your area. Then, personalize the seed packets by printing your names and date of wedding along with these words:

Love blossoms
As flowers do,
With tender care
It blooms anew!

This theme offers a freshness and charm that a wedding day deserves. Each part of the theme, like spring itself, is a reminder of simple pleasures and promised growth.

SUMMER TIME

Think of this theme as providing the best that su
A sampling of multiblooming flowers, sunlit fabri

settings will encourage your guests to relax and enjoy themselves on this eventful day,

The dictionary defines tulle as a tiny-meshed netting of silk, cotton, or synthetic. You'll define it as an easy way to achieve a breezy, summer-day look. This gauzy fabric, in colors kissed by the sun, will help solve many of your decorating questions throughout the wedding day.

Chances are, you'll be able to find bridal and bridesmaid dresses in tulle and lace overskirts. If not, then organza or dotted swiss come close to achieving the same look. Headpieces should be made of the same fabric.

Bouquets of fresh, airy, dainty summer flowers will complete the light, summer look. Choose from Queen Anne's lace, bachelor buttons, delphinium, candy tuft, and phlox. You could have the florist work small pieces of tulle, color matched to the bridesmaids' dresses, into the bouquets.

Dress the tables with clouds of light, billowy tulle. Spread a length of tulle over the center of a table that is already covered with a floor length tablecloth. Loosely tie the tulle into a generous knot at the center. Then nestle a large glass vase of summer flowers in the center of the knot. Scatter a few fresh or silk flower buds among the folds of the tulle.

In addition to the large centerpiece, collect small rosebud vases, and set these between every two place settings. Inexpensive bud vases will do, because they will be wrapped with color-coordinated ribbons. Start at the top of the vase and wind both ends of the ribbon around to the bottom. Finish off with a bow.

Knot a length of tulle and place it on the cake table just as you did for the dining tables. Set the wedding cake in the center of the knot and scatter flower buds about the folds. The cake itself should be seasonal. Choose a filling that echoes summer tastes. For example, a raspberry mousse filling is moist, light, and delicious.

Make your own favors by cutting small squares of tulle fabric and fill with summer-scented potpourri. Tie together, hobo style. These fragrant favors can be used as closet fresheners or tossed among your guests' bed pillows, leaving a lasting impression of your wedding day.

A white lattice screen wrapped with real or silk ivy will complete the cool, summery look. The screen will work well as a garden setting backdrop for the cake cutting ceremony and later for informal snaps of you and your guests.

There's no need to worry about hours of preparation time taking you away from fun-filled summer days. This easy theme gives you the freedom to enjoy the hazy, lazy days of summer and still have a beautiful wedding!

AUTUMN HARVEST

Fall back on gorgeous autumn leaves, bountiful harvests, and clear blue skies for this wedding theme. The autumn season offers a wide range of Mother Nature's treasures for inspiration. It's a time for social gathering, to give thanks, and to celebrate . . . your wedding!

Gather autumn leaves or, better still, use the craft store variety, the kind preserved with glycerine. The glycerine leaves won't dry up and become crisp and hard to handle. The first project you'll need the leaves for are pew markers. Make a mini-bouquet of leaves, add a creative twist of raffia ribbon bow, and tape the bouquet on the pews. (See Attaching Pew Markers, in the decoration for the Ceremony Guide.)

Use the leaves, too, as background for the centerpieces. Don't be stingy. Use plenty of leaves to cushion floral vases unique to the autumn season . . . garden pumpkins. Find medium to large Halloween-type pumpkins, slice off the top (about one-fourth of the way down), and scoop out the pulp. Set arrangements of chrysanthemums, cattails, and dried grasses in the pumpkins.

Apples can be pressed into centerpiece service, too. Insert small plastic candleholders (found at craft or floral shops) into the tops of apples. Fit tapered candles into these holders and finish with a twist of ribbon around the candle, close to the holder in the apple. The ribbon will add extra color while camouflaging the plastic handle.

Finish dressing the table with more fall leaves. Roll folded napkins into a cylinder shape and top each napkin with one leaf. Tie the leaf in place with more raffia ribbon.

There's no reason not to continue the autumn look with the wedding cake. Choose chysanthemums to decorate your cake. They are an especially hardy flower and will stay fresh looking without water for most of the day. If you've chosen a layer cake, accent each layer, as well as the cake top, with the flowers. Scatter fall leaves at the base of the cake. One last thought about the wedding cake: Although white cake is traditional, an old-fashioned spice cake makes an unexpected taste treat that is appropriate for the autumn season.

The selection of colors for a wedding depends on personal preference, but this season seems to inspire certain warm colors. Think in terms of peach, bittersweet, eggshell, brown, or rust to strike the right vibrant fall tone.

Let your invitations reflect fall colors, too. Choose a cream-colored paper with brown ink. Then, select a bright color such as peach or bittersweet for the lining of the envelope.

Add whimsical touches, if you would like, such as carved pumpkins, ceramic or plush squirrels, or stalks of corn. These reminders of autumn will bring a festive, seasonal look to your wedding.

WINTER GARDEN

This theme sets out to prove that winter weddings can provide an arborlike respite from the chilly weather outside. All your efforts will be targeted toward one goal . . . making a warm and cozy garden setting.

Take the chill out of the day as soon as possible, with cups of hot coffee, chocolate, or cider. This is easily accomplished if you set up a portable serving cart (with permission) inside the entrance to your church or temple. Here, guests can easily help themselves before the ceremony. Detail younger members of the family to see that there are enough clean cups, spoons, sugar, and so on for everyone.

Inside, create bright spots of color to warm the eye. Line the ceremony area with pots of tulips, daffodils, hyacinths, and narcissus. Skip
because they are too tiny to be effective. Tie wide ribbons
pots and finish with large bows. Extend the potted flowers
too.

Flowering spring bulbs are great for this theme because they are readily available at this time of year. Also, they can be moved from ceremony to reception with less chance of damage from the cold weather.

Make arrangements in November with your florist or greenhouse about the number of flowers you think you'll need. If you have a green thumb and have the room, you can plant the bulbs yourself. Just remember this . . . bulbs need to be chilled before planting in the fall. Get full how-to instructions when purchasing the bulbs.

Lovely everlasting flower bouquets seem to have been especially designed for the winter bride. Keep the flowering spring bulb theme by using everlasting tulips, daffodils, and so on. The shape, style, or color of bouquet is your choice.

Welcome your guests with a floral arbor set up at the entrance of your reception. Entwine garlands of smilax and orange blossoms around the arbor. Rent potted ficus trees to fill in empty spots and set pots of ferns on the floor, anywhere and everywhere. Outline the dance floor and other special areas with boxes of flowering bulbs.

Take this fantasy setting one step further with a rented indoor water fountain—an optional idea worth pursuing. Before deciding where to put the fountain, find out how much noise the fountain will make. You don't want the sound of dripping water to drown out conversation.

Plan centerpieces of small pots of flowering bulbs. Group varying heights of flowers together. Set some potted bulbs on upside-down pots and plant some bulbs in low, clay saucers. Trim all the containers with bright ribbon and large bows.

Timing is everything when working with flowering bulbs. For instance, if the blooms are only partially open on the day of the wedding, it will take about five hours to have them completely open. So it makes sense to put the partially opened flowers in a warm room early on the day of your wedding.

Now you have a way to provide an unexpected treat for your guests on a cold winter's day. Even in the heart of winter, this theme transports your guests to a carefree, warm, garden setting, making it a pleasure to celebrate your wedding.

Special
10. Site
Themes

A ren't possibilities wonderful, especially when it comes to choosing a location for your wedding? Read about each potential site and decide which theme best fits your wedding dreams.

BANQUET ROOM

This theme can turn the hotel, catering hall, private club, even a small-town school gymnasium into a festive, wedding-celebration look. The ability of these places to serve large crowds of people outweighs the disadvantage of working with a cold, impersonal room. It's important to start searching for this kind of site at least six months in advance; for popular clubs and hotel you may need to book at least a year in advance.

To make a large space seem inviting, fill the space with greenery and flowers. Another help is to rent only the amount of space you need. A slightly crowded room is better than having people rattle about in too large a space.

Decorate your site judiciously with plants and flowers. How to starkness of a long narrow passageway? Rent 8-foot m with tiny white lights, and set in the hall. Set off ropes of fresh flowers and greens. Place a fresh ers in the women's room. It's the little things that

An eye-catching ice sculpture of a flower basket in the center of your reception area will be noticed, too. If a summer wedding, fill the ice basket with yellow roses, Queen Anne's lace, and snapdragons. If the service people of your facility can't provide the ice sculpture, try your nearest vocational school. Students or recent graduates may be happy for the opportunity and are often-neglected creative resources.

Display your wedding cake off to one side of the room. Order alternate layers of strawberry and chocolate cake decorated with off-white lattice-worked frosting. Arrange fresh ivy between the tiered layers and top the cake with fresh flowers. Set two flower-basket shaped cakes decorated with flowers of spun sugar off to each side of the cake. Sweet peas, roses, or any kind of flower can be made of spun sugar.

The tables holding the wedding cake and ice sculpture should have floor length tablecloths. Drape ropings of smilax around the tables and at each top point of the draping, tack small bouquets of yellow roses.

Round tables with eight place settings are comfortable for sit-down dining. A large table creates too much distance across the table for good conversation. On the other hand, forcing ten or twelve place settings on a table for eight will crowd your guests.

Cover the tables with linen tablecloths and set floral centerpieces and votive candles in the center. Fancy folded napkins set on the table or tucked into glassware will lead all eyes to the table. A good book to find unique napkin folds is *Folding Table Napkins* (See Napkin Folding Book Source, in the Table Setting Guide for ordering details).

Usually the pre-dinner cocktails are served in a separate room, on an outside veranda, or at least to one side of the dining area. Small tables and some chairs for seating should be provided. Place smaller versions of the dinner centerpieces on these tables.

Though your reception site may seem large and impersonal, this theme can turn it into a warm and festive size. So don't hesitate an instant. Invite that large gang to help you celebrate your happy day.

AT HOME

Considering a home wedding? This theme shows you how to have the wedding of your dreams with all the trimmings in the comparative small space of your home. It is simply a matter of determining available space and then adjusting your invitation list.

In addition to the usual wedding list of things to do you'll need to think about taking care of a large group of people. For example, how is parking availability? Is there adequate space for parking, for both guests and service people? Check your toilet facilities. If necessary, you can rent porta johns. Also, your electrical service may be fine for your usual family needs, but will it handle kitchen equipment, lights, stereo, loudspeaker, and so on, all at one time?

Careful planning includes finding a place for everything. Since a home wedding means guests are invited to both the ceremony and the reception, draw a blueprint to take care of everyone all through the day. The ceremony itself should be in the loveliest area of your home. After that, choose areas for the buffet and cake table, coat storage, perhaps a room where the wedding party will dress, and so on.

Before you begin to decorate these areas, decide on a common theme. In other words, use the same style or colors for all the wedding fixings and trimmings. Outline the ceremony area simply, by setting candles and potted plants in a semicircle. Use rope swags to create an aisle for the wedding march. Decorate the swags with flower garlands and streamers of ribbons.

Don't make the mistake of ordering formal centerpieces. In this case, they're space wasters. Use small baskets of flowers or single-stemmed flowers in bud vases, instead. Garnish with ribbon. If your walls have cracks in them, bring in rental pictures to hide them. It's sneaky, but it does the job decoratively.

Keep the refreshments simple. Since a full bar takes up too much room as well as demanding a professional bartender, serve a choice of champagne, punch, and bottled water. Because the choice of refreshments is minimal, you can hire two or three college kids to do the serving. Decorate the punch bowl with tiny rosebuds floating on top and frozen in ice cubes.

Again, because space is at a premium, consider one violin or harp as opposed to a string quartet. Taped music for the ceremony and reception is another space-saving idea. Rent a recorder and tape the music you prefer.

Depending on the size of your home, you can serve anything from a cocktail and dessert buffet to a sit-down dinner. If it's to be a sit-down dinner, you'll have to seat guests in several different rooms. Mix and match your linen, dinnerware, flatware, and glassware. If you still don't have enough, see if the caterer can provide some of the pieces. Set small vases of garden flowers on the tables for a warm, at-home feeling.

A home setting is a delightful and intimate choice for your wedding. After all, if home is where the heart is, then home is the logical place for two hearts to be joined as one.

LAWN AND GARDEN

When scheduling a wedding for the warmer months of the year, one's thoughts tend to play with the idea of a garden wedding. If you enjoy being surrounded by natural beauty, seriously consider this theme for your wedding. Don't let the threat of rain stand in your way. There are ways to protect your celebration from the dampening effects of bad weather.

Site possibilities include your own backyard, Aunt Suzie's fabulous rock garden, a lush botanical garden, a serene city park, or the grounds of a historical mission. Do you live in a large city? Then search for rooftop gardens. To find unique locations, contact your local chamber of commerce, park commission, and historical society. Ask your friends and relatives, too. Personal recommendations are always a good way to find a reliable site.

In case of bad weather, provide a safety net for yourself. Set up food and beverages inside the house or in a rental tent. That way, there will be no wild dash to save the food, and the guests can simply move inside. Tents come with side panels and window flaps that can be put down quickly. Reserve a tent at least six months in advance, but first find out if you need a permit. Some cities require a permit even if you use your own backyard.

There are several ways to beat a weather crisis. Assuming you have rented a tent, bring in propane heaters for a damp day or cool summer night. On the other hand, you may have to rent fans or air conditioners to find relief from a heat wave. If a sudden shower should come up just before the ceremony, start the cocktail hour instead, under shelter, of course. Flexibility is the key word here. And finally, if you wake up to a water-soaked lawn, spread hay over the area so guests can stand on something dry.

Tents come in colors and stripes of all sizes. White tents are popular because they provide a neutral background for wedding colors. Wind garlands of myrtle, asparagus ferns, and tiny white lights around the supporting poles of the tent. Fix oasis cages of fern fronds to the bottom of the poles and around the stakes. Then set pots of plumeria or sweet william about for color.

At the risk of sounding too practical, think about wearing a tea length or short dress for a garden wedding. Because you will be primarily on garden paths and grass, you can see how a long, trailing train is likely to become dirty and grass stained. Rather than looking like the bride of the hour, you'll end up looking bedraggled.

The right style of shoes is important, too. Consider low heels or ballerina shoes for graceful walking. High heels will catch in the grass or the cracks in walkways. Do you really want a bridesmaid spiked forever into the lawn?

To keep everyone in a romantic lawn and garden party spirit, hire strolling musicians to wander about. Larger groups of musicians will need a platform and chairs to perform. You won't need to find chairs for taped music, but you will need loudspeakers and the necessary wiring. All can be obtained from rental companies. Even platform decks can be rented for your dancing enjoyment.

Planning a lawn and garden wedding may seem like you're daring the gods. But contingency planning can take most of the risk element away. Imagine how your wedding will benefit from the relaxing qualities of flowers in bloom, green grass, and fresh air.

POOLSIDE

A reception planned for poolside can turn an ordinary wedding into a summer's event. You'll have no trouble finding the right ingredients for this theme. Take one pool, some festive food and drink, a sprinkling of bright and breezy decorations, and stir together. Add good company and you have the fixings for a refreshing celebration.

You can add to the enjoyment of the pool setting by adding unexpected decorative touches. Use childrens' safety rings to float fresh flowers in the pool. Nestle plastic containers of flowers inside the rings. Or tie bunches of balloons to the rings, letting the breeze take them where they will. (See more about this in . . . as in Poolside, in the Decorations for the Reception Guide.)

As night falls, bathe the pool in light from floating candles. Keep the candles in one place with weights obtained from a pool supply store. Add romantic light around the pool with twinkling Japanese lanterns that sway softly in the breeze.

The table settings set up around the pool should continue the light, casual mood. Rent tables and wooden folding chairs, preferably white chairs. Cover the tables with awning-striped fabric. Use casual arrangements of flowers in plastic vases in a wide range of colors. Anchor the lightweight, plastic vases by dropping florist pebbles in the bottom.

Use the same striped tablecloths on the buffet tables. Tuck in galax leaves and palm fronds around the serving dishes. Elegant watermelon swans, cantaloupe baskets, and pineapple boats make good cold food servers. Serve hot foods in silver serving dishes.

Offer refreshments in plastic glasses. Garnish the drinks with paper umbrellas, fruit spears, and decorative straws. Shop your import stores for these items.

Serving poolside is one occasion when plastic is not only acceptable but required for safety reasons. Several kinds are available. If you need plastic champagne glasses beware the ones that have removable bases. Sometimes the base falls off, spilling the champagne.

If you have hired a catering company, ask the staff to dress in casual costumes for an outdoor pool setting theme. Simple striped T-shirts, using the same colors that are in the tablecloths, worn with white pants and any white sport shoes make a jaunty and colorful addition to the celebration. You or the caterer can provide the decorative T-shirts.

Favors for the guests can be packaged in stripes, as well. Cut squares of striped fabric with pinking shears. Fill the center of the squares with Jordan almonds. Then gather the ends of the square together and tie with white ribbon. Place a favor at each place setting.

When it's time for the traditional rice throwing, blow bubbles instead to signify best wishes for a good life. Give your guests jars of bubble water, tied with ribbons. It's pretty and it's fun. Besides, everyone will be outside, so you don't have to worry about wet rugs, sticky upholstery, and so on.

This theme turns a pool area into a dream site of unabashed prettiness. Your guests will enjoy the sophisticated yet casual atmosphere that only this setting can give to a celebration.

SCENIC SETTING

Picture the natural beauty and splendor of a mountaintop setting as a background for your wedding. This is just one of many dramatic sites available at national or state parks. If you, as a couple, enjoy the grandeur of the great outdoors, look for a scenic site in a park near you. Once the perfect locale is found, then proceed as in any other wedding . . . except for one slight difference—everything must be portable.

Before you start backpacking in your supplies, reserve your park setting. This should be done well in advance of the wedding date, especially if you have a certain spot in mind. Find out the guidelines that must be observed. For example, what are the park hours and beverage restrictions? Are there cooking facilities, or must all the food be prepared beforehand?

Whether your site is remote or close to a parking area, you'll still need to focus on easy-to-handle wedding fixings. Keep the decorations simple. Plenty of lavender and white ribbon to tie bows on trees is more than enough. The unexpectedness of satin bows decorating trees, bark and all, catches the spirit of this kind of wedding.

Because you have abundant nature available, any elaborate flower arrangements are unnecessary. Instead, do something fun with the wild flowers nearby. Put together centerpieces of watermelon and wild flowers. Bring halved watermelons and an ice pick to poke holes in the melon for flower stems. Stick the flower stems down into the fruit. If wildflowers are unavailable, substitute garden flowers.

As for refreshments, a simple menu works best in this setting. Serve meat and cheese trays, watermelon baskets, vegetable trays and lavender punch, matching the lavender and white ribbons decorating the trees. (See Lavender Punch, Decorative Recipe Guide.) Everything but the punch can be ordered from the deli.

This picnic-style service can be altered slightly by packing individual lunches. Purchase glossy, lavender, lunch-size bags. After the lunch is packed, tie with white ribbon and a sprig of plum blossoms (or any sweet-smelling blossoms). Set the bags on a table with extra sandwich servings, condiments, and refreshments.

As for the ceremony itself, select the best possible view. Don't be bashful about arranging a dramatic space for your exchanging of vows. If possible, time the ceremony for sunset and let Nature do her stuff. The birds will be in evening song at this time, also. The sound of birds singing may not be the same as an organ, but the music is still wonderful in its own way.

A real advantage of this site, besides the grand vista, is the wealth of picture-taking possibilities. When choosing a spot for the wedding photos, look for focal points like a moss-covered wall, a large jutting rock, or a majestic tree. Don't take your setting for granted. Other couples drive miles for the kind of background you'll have at hand.

This type of wedding works best with a certain kind of couple. But if you think an outdoor setting is for you, then make the arrangements, issue the invitations, and enjoy the kind of celebration a charming scenic site has to offer.

11. Today's Ceremony Themes

T hese themes are intended to show the variety of ceremonies available to you. Consider your situation and style, then go ahead and plan the kind of ceremony that seems right for you.

INFORMAL DAY

Think of this theme as providing a small, intimate jewel of a daytime wedding celebration. The ceremony, in keeping with a small group of guests and an informal style, usually takes place in the home, a chapel, or a private club. The reception is held in the home, restaurant, or parklike setting. Since you won't have to plan in quantity, you can concentrate on quality for all the details of your wedding.

Because this is an informal wedding, invitations sent in your best handwritten style on good-quality paper is not only acceptable but personally elegant as well. And, because there is a limited number of guests, the task of writing invitations can be reasonably carried out.

The guidelines for a properly written invitation suggest the use of the phrase "The pleasure of your company is requested . . ." when ceremonies take place in secular places like the home, club, or hotel. "The honour of your presence is requested . . ." is used for religious ceremonies.

As the bride, you will set the fashion statement for your wedding. Wear a suit or street length dress in white or the color of your choice for this day. Carry a simple nosegay or a single stemmed flower, or wear a corsage. The groom wears a suit or dinner jacket with a white, colored, or striped shirt with a tie.

Ordinarily, there is only a maid of honor and one best man as attendants. They should follow your fashion lead. The maid of honor is given a bouquet of flowers to hold or a corsage to wear. Both the best man and the groom can wear a rosebud or other single blossom in their lapels.

If your reception is held at home or in a parklike setting, try this posh paper wedding setting. Layer the tables with paper table skirts and paper tablecloths. Tack large satin bows at every corner with streamers falling to the floor or ground.

Alternate floral patterns and matching colors of paper plates at each place setting. Then, sandwich a white paper doily between a large floral patterned plate and a small plate of a contrasting color. Display plastic flatware tied together with satin or paper ribbon bows and placed on floral printed paper napkins.

Serve champagne or sparkling water in plastic stemware. Reserve a few of the extra glasses for flower vases. Tie ribbon bows around the stems of these vases.

For favors a little different, but still in keeping with the paper table setting, put together spoonfuls of chocolate kisses. Wrap three chocolate kisses in a plastic soup spoon with nylon netting to match your table colors. Tie a matching ribbon around the loose ends of the netting and the handle of the spoon. Before tying, run one end of the ribbon through a paper bell with this piece of rhyming whimsy: "A spoonful of kisses brings lots of good wishes."

If you choose this small and informal, but intimate wedding, be assured you won't have to deal with a nagging feeling of missing out on something. You'll discover how a simple but quality wedding plan such as this will give you a feeling of being very special.

FORMAL EVENING

A formal wedding, the kind of wedding most young women dream about, involves an impressive ceremony, beautiful formal attire, a gala reception, and all the traditional touches one associates with weddings. Held after 6:00 P.M., a formal evening wedding accommodates between 100 and 300 people. Any wedding of this size demands a great amount of planning and coordination on your part.

Planning a wedding should begin with the selection of site, date, and time of the wedding. Only then can other tasks, such as sending invitations, be considered. For a more relaxed pace, invitations should be ordered at least three months ahead of time so they can be addressed, sealed, and mailed about four weeks before the wedding.

A formal wedding requires engraved invitations, traditionally worded, in black ink on white or ivory paper. Since engraving is very costly (letters are cut into the paper), most invitations are printed by a process called thermography (a heat process that fuses ink and powder). It resembles the raised letters of engraving.

A formal wedding also dictates the traditional long white wedding dress with long train and veil for the bride. Gloves or long sleeves are worn to cover the arm. Bridesmaid dresses are long or ankle length, with gloves optional.

The groom and his attendants wear black or gray tuxedos. Color is introduced through a rosebud or blossom (no baby's breath) pinned to the lapel. Between Memorial Day and Labor Day, it's acceptable to wear a classic white dinner jacket, black pants, and white shirt. As for the number of attendants, the common rule of thumb is one usher for every fifty guests. It's not necessary to have an equal number of bridesmaids.

Arrange for a general first meeting with your various services when everyone can attend. It's important to get these people together at the beginning of the planning session because the caterer may have some suggestions for the florist, the florist may suggest fresh flowers for the wedding cake, and so on. It's important, too, that everyone involved in the wedding plans have the same objective in mind in order to achieve a coordinated look.

A decorative theme look increases visual interest and personalizes the formal wedding just as it does for any wedding. The use of your initials (both bride and groom) as decoration illustrates this beautifully.

For example, your initials can be a part of the table centerpieces. Wind silk ivy leaves around a formed wire of your combined initials. Accent the ivy with white satin ribbon laced in and out, or tie a big satin bow at the base of the wire form. Baby's breath can be used in place of silk ivy.

Top your wedding cake with your initials, too. A smaller version of the wired silk ivy leaves can be used as a cake topper, or ask your cake service to make up sugared initials for the cake top.

Boxed favors for your guests can display your initials, also. Print your initials in large, black script directly on small gold boxes of candy, or seal the boxes with gold labels printed with your initials. Fill the boxes with delicious liquor truffles . . . perhaps one each of kahlua, amaretto, cognac, and creme de cacao flavors.

A wedding like this depends on careful planning and plenty of coordination. It's all worthwhile, though, because this wedding will reflect the fairytale quality of the wedding of your dreams.

Second Marriage

Here is a second chance to plan the wedding of your dreams . . . your way. Since you've gone through a wedding once before, your expectations will be closer to reality. Consequently, you can relax a little and plan the kind of wedding that will be meaningful and joyful for you.

Now that the two of you are planning a new life together, a fresh start, it truly is a time to celebrate. You can choose to mark this occasion with all the traditional customs, including a white bridal dress or not. Although ceremony protocol may not be as rigid as it was the first time around, you will most likely take more of a personal interest in the exchanging of vows and spend some time thinking about the kind of ceremony you want.

If you have children, it would be thoughtful and caring to have them participate as much as possible. For instance, young children can precede you down the aisle handing out tiny nosegays or dropping scented flower petals. Older children can take the role of attendants and join together with friends and family in loving support of your union.

They can handle the readings of the ceremony, hold the bouquet, and just generally be a part of things as much as possible.

The setting for the ceremony should present an atmosphere of warmth and good wishes also. This second wedding doesn't need to answer the rigid "Which side of the aisle do we sit on?" question. Let the guests come in and seat themselves anywhere they wish.

If folding chairs are used, set them up in three sections, with you and the wedding party in the center. You can create another kind of intimate setting by asking the guests to stand gathered around you during the ceremony. Have the officiant encourage the guests to come forward at the start of the ceremony.

When the ceremony is over, mingle with your guests and enjoy a little socializing. The receiving line and all its protocol are replaced by your warm greetings extended to small groups of guests. This serves to emphasize the casual warmth and happiness you want to share during this second wedding celebration.

A sit-down dinner can be as elegant or as casual as you want. If it's to be a dinner in a hall or hotel, group the tables around the wedding party table. Many caterers suggest this kind of arrangement for the sit-down wedding dinner. A center table is designated for the wedding party in place of a head table.

Don't bother with place cards if most of your guests are friends. Let them seat themselves as they would at a dinner party. They can meet and mingle as they wish.

After all, the general mood of this theme is relaxed and easygoing. A little thoughtfulness and courtesy applied to all aspects of this wedding will create warm and wonderful memories for everyone.

DOUBLE WEDDING

Here come the brides! Enjoy a celebration of two weddings almost for the price of one. If you have a friend or relative who is setting a wedding date close to yours, consider a double wedding. This theme shows you how you can share the spotlight comfortably and cut your wedding expense by half.

The positive benefit of a double wedding will more than outweigh any potential problems, since several expenses will be shared. For example, the cost of invitations, reception area rental, musicians, food and servers, table centerpieces, and other decorations can be shared. Even the photographer should cost less, since the two wedding parties will be at the same place.

Potential problems created by a double wedding can be worked out with a little foresight and planning. Discuss the style of wedding each of you would like before making any commitments. Once the kind of wedding has been decided on, you can think about details such as the color of dresses, the kinds of decorations, and the protocol.

Try to choose colors that complement or contrast with each other. Then each bride can use a favorite color for "her" attendants' dresses as well as the wedding decorations, without the problem of colors clashing.

Any logistical problems such as who walks down the aisle first or who says their vows first can be solved by drawing straws. Should the brides share the same father, he would simply walk one bride down the aisle and then go back and repeat the ceremony with the second bride. An alternative is to have each couple walk down the aisle together, one ahead of the other.

A table setting especially suited for double weddings can be relatively simple. Arrange colorful floral centerpieces flanked by tall white candles. Then wind narrow satin ribbons, in each bride's colors, around the candleholder and down on the table.

Alternate napkin colors at each place setting. If you personalize the napkins, put both sets of names on each napkin. And remember, anything you would personalize for a one-couple wedding can be personalized with both sets of names. Napkins, candy boxes, grooms' cake boxes, and cake bags are some possibilities.

Another way to highlight but still unify the double wedding table setting is with this wedding favor idea Tie crinkle ribbon around two lollipops. Glue paper hearts with your names on each tip of the ribbon end. (See Double Lollipop Favor, Favor Guide, for how-to directions.)

Though you will be sharing many things throughout the day, you should have separate wedding cakes. Two cakes means you can have the cake of your choice plus the opportunity to save the top layer as a keepsake cake for your first anniversary. Serve half portions so each guest can have a taste of both cakes.

Still hesitating about a double wedding? Then look at it this way. If something awful happens during the wedding, you'll have someone to share your pain. And if all goes well, you'll have a doubly delightful wedding day!

CIVIL CEREMONY

This theme is an alternative to the religious ceremony. The civil ceremony can be as short and simple or elaborately paced as you prefer. This holds true for the reception following the ceremony, as well. Just because you choose not to marry in the traditional way doesn't mean you can't celebrate in the style to which you would like to be accustomed.

The ceremony can take place in a judge's chambers, in the county clerk's office, at home, at a park site, or in a hotel. (Officials who can perform ceremonies vary from state to state.) Whether the official is a family friend or a stranger, you can personalize the ceremony if you plan ahead of time. Talk to the person who will be officiating about your plans so enough time is scheduled for the kind of ceremony you would like to have.

The usual civil ceremony is brief and to the point, maybe a bit briefer than you would like. Consider, then, the addition of a favorite poem or parts of a lyric to make the ceremony more meaningful to you. A few words of promise, spoken spontaneously by you and the groom, would add immeasurably to the moment.

Dress can be as formal or informal as you would like. If your ceremony is to take place at city hall, you may be more comfortable in a daytime length dress or suit. Then if you wish, you can change into a formal dress for your reception. If the wedding takes place in a home or hotel, there is no reason not to wear a formal bridal dress.

The bridal bouquet should follow the style of the dress. A corsage or small bouquet of flowers is appropriate even if the ceremony is held in the county clerk's office.

An informal wedding held in the county clerk's office or the judge's chamber requires only a maid of honor and a best man. It is possible to ask employees in the office to witness your marriage, also.

Invitations are always nice when printed, but here again, it depends on the style of your wedding. You can write short personal notes inviting a select few to the ceremony and extend printed invitations to a larger group to attend the reception. Follow the same advice in choosing invitations as you would for a religious ceremony.

The reception following the ceremony can be held at a hotel, private club, restaurant, home, or park. You can invite just a few friends or a large gathering of friends and family to help you celebrate this occasion. If, for example, you want a partylike theme for your reception, simply take a look at some of the ideas offered in other chapters and draw up your plans accordingly.

As you can see, the civil ceremony lends itself to several possibilities. Whether you go formal or informal, large or small guest list, you'll enjoy a memorable wedding made to order for you.

REAFFIRMATION

This theme celebrates your marriage with a renewal of your wedding vows. Since this is a replay, you can be more relaxed about the whole affair, both in attitude and entertaining style. Whether you decide to celebrate formally or informally, this day will be a nostalgic memory trip reaffirming the future. By all means, include your children in the ceremony as well as in the planning stages.

Decide on a celebration that will have special meaning to you. You may elect to have a formal ceremony officiated by a minister, rabbi, or priest. Or, simply choose to exchange a few meaningful words in front of close friends and family at home. In any case, this time the planning process will benefit from your combined shared experience.

Once you've decided on the kind of celebration you would like, it's time to plan the invitations. If the children are old enough, they may want to formally announce the reaffirmation by their parents. Then again, you may simply opt for some handwritten personal notes to a few special people. Whether formal or casual, the invitations should tell your guests of your reaffirmation plans, let them know the time of the ceremony, and indicate how formal the dress should be.

In this ceremony, secular or religious, you will renew your vows to one another. You can choose a well-known passage from the Bible or a special love poem shared in the years you've been together. another choice is to write your own special affirmation. This will give you the chance to give special recognition to your children and to your guests.

Accessories and decorations should follow the theme of your ceremony. Since this is a repeat performance, include any memorabilia from the original wedding. It'll be a decorative plus.

Old wedding pictures are always fun to look at. They can be blown up and set on tables or hung on walls. If you have children, include them in this memory decor, too, by placing their pictures next to the wedding pictures.

The bridal nosegay can be resurrected and incorporated into a fresh bouquet by a florist. Of course, your wedding dress can be displayed along with any other accessories, both yours and your husband's.

Food can also be a complete or partial duplicate of your wedding repast. However, if you've decided on a certain theme, match the menu to the ambience of the theme. For example, if you are celebrating in an outdoor setting, provide a picnic menu. If a romantic Victorian setting, serve petit fours and coffee or tea.

If you prefer that your guests do not bring gifts, you can ask them for expressions of heartfelt sentiment. Short notes or special poems or passages can be shared at a set time during the ceremony.

On the other hand, you may want to gift your guests. These can take the form of party favors. For some fresh ideas, look over the list of suggestions in the Favor Guide.

Fashion for this affair is up to you. You can wear formal attire or a dress that can be worn for other occasions. Your attendants can follow your lead. If bridesmaids wear different dress styles and colors, the best way to achieve a cohesive look is to purchase similar bouquets for you and them.

This theme is a real opportunity to recognize in a public way the love and support between the two of you. It's a time of well-deserved celebration, to be enjoyed by all.

Wedding
12. Plan
List

Be prepared for your wedding. A wedding plan can, at a glance, show you what needs to be done as well as give you a sense of accomplishment for tasks already finished. Any nervous anticipation you may experience can be put to rest if you keep your plan nearby. After all, there's nothing like careful planning to soothe those jangled nerves.

FIRST THINGS FIRST

- Think about and decide on what kind of wedding you would like to have.
- Try to estimate number of guests that will be invited from both families.
- Make a decision about the reception site as soon as possible. Some popular halls and hotels are reserved up to a year in advance.
- Once the site is reserved, find a caterer who is available for the wedding day, that is, if a kitchen staff from the site isn't available. Some caterers are booked well in advance, as well.
- Make an appointment with an official at your church or temple to discuss the date and time of the wedding.
- Order your wedding dress now. If you're going to sew or have the dress made, buy the fabric and pattern as soon as possible.
- Get the bridesmaids together and shop for dresses. If the dresses are to be sewn, buy fabric and patterns as soon as possible.

- Reserve a photographer for the specific time and date of the wedding.
- If you're determined to have a popular band play at your wedding, you'll need to make arrangements with them well ahead of time, sometimes months ahead. This goes for disc jockeys, too.

THREE MONTHS BEFORE THE WEDDING

- Order invitations you will need, plus a few extras.
- Start a card file on the wedding party and guests. List name, address, and the telephone number of each member of the wedding party.
- Order tuxedos for the groom and attendants.
- After the wedding party attire has been chosen, find a florist whose work you like and who is available on your wedding day.
- Any music, other than what your church or temple provides, should be chosen, and musicians or vocalists engaged for the wedding date. Most likely, you will be working with a director of music. He or she is there to help you, so give them enough time to plan the music for your ceremony.
- Transportation for the wedding party, if rented, should be reserved.
- If you need to hire someone for the audio or video recordings, make the arrangements now. It's also possible to rent the equipment and ask a friend to take charge on the day of the wedding.

FOUR WEEKS BEFORE THE WEDDING

- Complete the guest card file and mail all the invitations.
- Purchase favors for your guests or buy the materials needed to make them, and plan a pre-wedding craft party.
- Select gifts for the wedding party attendants.
- Order the wedding cake from the bakery.
- Reserve rooms for your guests who need overnight lodging.

- At the same time, arrange to have guests met if they are arriving by plane.
- If necessary, arrange for guest parking and a parking attendant.
- Everyone should be sure to make the final fitting date for the bridal dress and bridesmaids' dresses.
- Shop for a wedding guest book.

TWO WEEKS BEFORE THE WEDDING

- Complete the wedding forms for newspaper announcements.
- Pick up the marriage license.
- Put the finishing touches on any wedding decorations, favors, and so on, that you are doing yourself.
- Start writing thank-you notes for gifts you have already received.
- Tell wedding party attendants when and where they need to be for photographs.

LAST WEEK

- Arrange for pickup of any rental equipment.
- Give final guest count to the caterer.
- Double-check arrangements with the photographer. Make a list of must-have pictures.
- Double-check on the florist.
- Double-check musicians and list any reception activities they should announce. Make sure they have a list of special dances, including how you want the names to be announced. Make any special requests now.
- Double-check the bakery and give instructions as to where and what time the wedding cake should be delivered.
- Pick up tuxedos.
- Make up an emergency kit to take to the ceremony. Make sure you have hairpins, lipstick, lotion, a pair of flat shoes, stockings, needle and thread, comb, and so on.

Atten
13.   Gift
Guide

S eemingly a simple task, gifting the attendants turns out to be in many cases a knotty problem. You'll be sure to find a solution, exactly suited to your wedding and attendants, in this list of suggestions.

- Jewelry is always a popular and welcome gift. Choose jewelry that will complement your theme . . . as in Gifts from the Sea, Northeast Region, Northwest Region, Southwest Region, Victorian Delight, and Fabulous Fifties.
- Eye-catching beverage containers such as etched glasses, hand-blown goblets, and pewter mugs are very giftable and can be used right away at the reception . . . as in Puck's Perfect Party and Medieval "Marry" Making.
- Personal grooming and dress accessories as gifts are always a good choice. Such items as crocheted gloves, combs, and umbrellas are some ideas that fit easily into themes . . . as in I Love Country, Parasol Style, and Old Mexico.
- Home or office items offer a variety of gift solutions. Consider address book, picture frame, sleigh bell ribbon, terra cotta sun wall hanging, sun catcher, velvet and lace potpourri heart, or fountain pen and bottle of ink . . . as in Casual Chic, Northwest Region, Southwest Region, The Great Gatsby, and Hearts & Flowers.

- Everyone enjoys receiving a personalized gift. Give candleholders etched with their initials, embroidered handkerchiefs, miniature crafted ships with their name painted on the side . . . as in Light up the Night, I Love Country, and Northwest Region.
- Try this noteworthy idea. Write a short personal note to accompany the gift. It will make the gift and moment more meaningful . . . as in South Region, Fabulous Fifties, and Fanfare.
- Food-related gifts are tasty and tasteful. You can make up giftable packages of nuts, fruits, and candy or small selections of chocolate, tea, or coffee . . . as in Giving Thanks, Romantic Renaissance, and Midwest Region.
- Your attendants will enjoy entertaining gifts such as books, theater tickets, and tapes or records . . . as in New York, New York!
- Charms that are engraved easily solve the gift question . . . as in South Region and Jamaica Bound.
- For just plain fun, give inflatable drink holders, funny umbrellas, or imprinted T-shirts . . . as in Parasol Style and Key Largo.

Invitation
14. Guide

W hether casual or formal, invitations are meant to extend a heartfelt wish that your guests share the joy and celebration of your marriage. One of these ideas will be sure to set the stage for your wedding theme.

- Add artwork to any part of your invitation, depicting the theme of your wedding . . . as in Fanfare, Parasol Style, and Romantic Renaissance.
- Invitations can set the mood of the wedding simply by their print style. For example, a modern print hints of a contemporary wedding. On the other hand, an Old English style written in calligraphy on parchment paper speaks of quite a different kind of wedding . . . as in Contemporary Drama and Medieval "Marry" Making.
- Include a tangible taste of your theme in the invitation envelope. It could be a pressed rose, rose petals, a sprinkling of tiny paper hearts or stars, or miniature paper flags . . . as in The Great Gatsby, Hearts & Flowers, and Flag-Waving Festival.
- Invitations with a bit of color added to them suggests a gay, informal wedding. Choose red ink on pink paper or line a cream-colored envelope with peach or bittersweet . . . as in Hearts & Flowers and Autumn Harvest.

- Invitations can be printed by fine stationery houses or simply written in your best handwritten style on good-quality paper . . . as in Informal Day.
- Guidelines for a properly written invitation suggest the use of the phrase "The pleasure of your company is requested . . . " This phrasing is used when ceremonies take place in secular places like the home, a club, or a hotel. "The honour of your presence is requested . . . " is used for religious ceremonies . . . as in Informal Day.
- A formal wedding requires engraved invitations, traditionally worded, in black ink on white or ivory paper . . . as in Formal Evening.

15.
Centerpiece
Guide

If you do nothing else decoratively, it's important to highlight your tables. Centerpieces for your table can be floral or otherwise. You'll find a little of both in the following suggestions.

- Add extra height to floral centerpieces by attaching balloons. You'll get more punch for the money. Tie 1/10-inch ribbons to the necks of the balloons and let the ribbons curl down naturally . . . as in Balloon Bash.

- Find ideas for unique centerpieces off the decorative beaten track. For example, a pet shop trip can yield interesting results. Everyone will enjoy the unexpected bubble bowls of fish set in the center of their table . . . as in Gifts from the Sea.

Gifts from the Sea Centerpiece
as in Gifts from the Sea

Set a small bubble bowl on one side of a flat plastic dish (in gold, silver, or a color). Put a layer of loose, simulated, white pearls in the bottom of the bowl, add water, and goldfish (beta fish are bred to survive in small amounts of water, too). Hot-glue a floral foam brick (one-fourth of the brick) on the other side of the plastic dish. Cover the foam with moss and stick a few curly willow branches into the foam. Drape a strand of pearls (buy strands of pearls by the yard at craft stores) on the willow and down into the fishbowl. Sprinkle seashells on the bottom of the plastic dish. For added color, hot-glue tiny silk blossoms to the willow branches.

- Highlight arrangements of flowers and ribbons with decorative elements such as fans and parasol . . . as in Fanfare and Parasol Style.
- An imaginative background adds to the total look of the centerpiece. Try things like straw hats, sombreros, sand-filled saucers, or mirror squares . . . as in I Love Country, Old Mexico, Key Largo, and Light up the Night.
- Nature is always ready to lend her bounty to the centerpiece with evergreen, pine cones, tropical flowers, autumn leaves, and pumpkins . . . as in Northwest Region, Hawaiian Luau, and Autumn Harvest.
- Let candles take center stage in planning your centerpiece . . . as in Jamaica Bound and Light up the Night.
- Throw your hat into the centerpiece ring. Set sombreros with two or three roly poly lights in the wide brim on the table. Add a sprinkling of strawflowers. Or, fill the rim of a straw garden hat with daisies and zinnias. Tie a ribbon around the band of the hat and trail the streamers . . . as in Old Mexico and I Love Country.
- Art can be a great source for creative wedding centerpieces . . . as in South Region and Romantic Renaissance.

Della Robbia Centerpiece

. . . as in South Region

Use glass, brass, or silver compotes or trays as your base. Line the container with green leaves and then build fresh fruit into a pyramid. Attach the fruit with small wood picks dipped in oil of cloves. The oil of cloves will prevent the fruit from decaying around the wood picks. Top the pyramid with a small pineapple.

- All kinds of containers can set off a centerpiece to perfection. Some ideas include a fireside basket, an inexpensive, painted glass vase, and a terra cotta piece . . . as in Spring Is Here, The Great Gatsby, and Southwest Region.

Fireside Basket Centerpiece
. . . as in Spring Is Here

Select open-ended, oval base baskets with handles, the kind used to carry firewood. Spray the basket with a whitewash spray. The spray, available at craft stores, comes in blue, pink, or white and gives the basket a transparent paint look. Hot-glue a child's sprinkling can to the bottom of the basket. This will be the vase for a bouquet of daisies. Fill in the rest of the basket with florist moss. Add packets of garden seeds and some miniature garden tools to the arrangement. A bouquet of fresh daisies completes the centerpiece.

- Holiday weddings have a natural storehouse of centerpiece findings. Just borrow the holiday's decorations, such as red hearts, Easter grass, cardboard rockets, and glass ball tree ornaments . . . as in Hearts & Flowers, Easter Celebration, Flag-waving Festival, and Mistletoe & Poinsettia.

Patriotic Centerpiece
. . .as in Flag-Waving Festival

Purchase clay flowerpot saucers, one for each centerpiece. Paste a small paper cone to a cardboard about 5 inches long. (Use the tubes from wrapping paper rolls and so on.) Paint the rocket white with a red and blue design. Hot-glue the paper rocket to one side of the saucer. Position a chunk of foam on the other side and stick in three or four flowers. Fill out the centerpiece with onion grass. Onion grass is sometimes called silver exploding paper because tiny strips of foil seem to explode off the stems. You can curl the foil strips by running your fingers down the edges. Onion grass is available at craft or flower shops.

- Tie the centerpiece to the theme with any of its parts: Flowers, ribbons, or flower vase . . . as in Ethnic Food and Table Setting and Medieval "Marry" Making.
- Sometimes formal centerpieces aren't necessary. Instead, use baskets of flowers, wildflowers stuck into watermelon, garden

flowers in small vases, single blossoms in champagne glasses . . . as in At Home, Scenic Setting, and Informal Day.

- Stylized centerpieces can be made by entwining real or silk ivy around wire bent into recognizable forms . . . as in Formal Evening.
- Centerpieces can delight the eye and solve a sticky problem at the same time, such as in a double wedding with different color schemes . . . as in Double Wedding.
- Your florist can be a gold mine of information as far as suggesting and finding just the perfect accessory to complete a theme centerpiece. One florist was able to supply just the right size of flamingo . . . as in Key Largo.
- Use tulle, a light billowy material, to dress up your tables. Spread a length of tulle over the center of a table, already covered with a floor length tablecloth. Loosely tie the tulle into a generous knot at the center. Then, nestle a large glass vase of summer flowers into the center of the knot . . . as in Summer Time.
- Collect inexpensive bud vases, enough to set several at each table. Wrap the vases with color-coordinated ribbon. Start at the top of the vase and wind both ends of the ribbon around to the bottom. Finish off with a bow . . . as in Summer Time.
- Use mirrors as the base for candlelit centerpieces. Purchase packages of ten to twelve mirror squares from a lumber store. Set groupings of candles on the squares and wind opalescent ribbon in and around the candles. Scatter glitter and rhinestones over all . . . as in Light up the Night.
- Elevate centerpieces to achieve a dramatic effect. Use plastic pillars (any florist will know what you're talking about) for height and set white candles in clear roly polys underneath the flower arrangement. White dendrobriums give a sweeping spray look, while a few white roses and freesia tucked in exude a subtle fragrance. For greenery, add a pearlized grass called isolepsis . . . as in New York, New York!
- If you're planning a reception in a small area, don't use formal centerpieces. They're space wasters. Use small baskets of flowers

or single stemmed flowers in bud vases, in.
Home.

- Vegetables and fruit can give a boost to centerp.
Scoop out the pulp from pumpkins and set flowers i.
can serve as candleholders. Insert small plastic can
(found at craft or floral shops) into the tops of apples. h. ..ndles
into the holders . . . as in Autumn Harvest.
- Grapevine wreaths, wreaths made of birch branches, or any kind
of vine make whimsical centerpieces . . . as in Puck's Perfect
Party.

Grapevine Wreath
. . . as in Puck's Perfect Party

1. Cut any vine or pliable branch that is flexible when soaked.
Tendrils on the vine will make a more attractive wreath.
2. Soak vines overnight or as long as it takes to make vines flexible.
3. Have on hand a circular form to wind vines around. This can be
as small as a drinking glass (for wreaths intended to be used as
napkin rings) or as large as a garbage can. The most common
wreath size is 10 to 12 inches.
4. Wind vines around the form until you have several layers.
Various lengths of vines can be used because you will overlap
vines as you work.
5. Tie the wreath tightly with twine in four to six places. Let dry.
6. Lift the circular form out of the dried ring. At this stage, you may
want to remove the twine from a few places. The twine support
that is left should have the ends trimmed down to the knot.
7. Leave the vine wreath in its natural state and decorate with preserved baby's breath and a few dried or silk flowers.
8. The wreaths can also be spray painted any color, but the vines
must be totally dry or the paint won't adhere.

Table Setting
16. Guide

Design your own version of the well-dressed table. Attention to detail, perhaps an unexpected accessory, will create special eye appeal for your tables. Whether you're setting each table yourself or directing the table setting efforts of others, these suggestions will help you create a becoming table.

- Use lace, netting, or tulle to dress up your tables. For example, drape lace edging around the candleholders and tie bows on glassware stems. Tulle can be loosely tied into a generous knot at the center of the table, forming a filmy nest for a vase of flowers . . . as in Giving Thanks and Summer Time.
- Table settings can reflect your heritage. Embroidered ethnic tablecloths, champagne toasting glasses etched in the language of your choice, or serving pieces in the colors or design of your heritage can proudly display your ethnic background . . . as in Ethnic Food and Table Setting.
- Stir up distant vacation images with palm leaves, coconut serving pieces, serapes, or Caribbean blue table linen . . . as in Old Mexico and Key Largo.
- If you are going to supply the tableware, don't be afraid to mix and match. Today's table fashions lean toward the eclectic, allowing a more sensible approach to setting tables for large crowds . . . as in At Home.

- Let your table settings reflect the kind of reception you're having. Plastic and paperware are logical choices for outdoor weddings . . . as in Poolside, Scenic Setting, and Informal Day.
- The size of dining tables is important and should be considered in wedding planning. Round tables are best for good conversation. Eight place settings are a comfortable number. Too small a table will crowd eight people, whereas a large table will create too much distance between opposite place settings, inhibiting conversation . . . as in Banquet Room.
- Accent the tabletop with Mother Nature's help. Scatter autumn leaves, pine branches, and pine cones on the table as accents . . . as in Autumn Harvest and Northwest Region.
- Dramatic color combinations set a winning table. Select black tablecloths, instead of white, and contrast the black with red napkins, white floral centerpieces, or a single red rose . . . as in The Great Gatsby and New York, New York!
- Candleholders can add to the loveliness of your table theme. Some candleholders reflect a traditional or contemporary styling. Others display a whimsical creativity. For example, hollowed out tiny pumpkins or apples make inexpensive but eye-catching candleholders. Insert small plastic candleholders (found at craft or floral shops) into the tops . . . as in Autumn Harvest.
- Napkin rings are a special addition to the table, whether the ring is a simple ribbon or something more substantial, such as papier mâché fruit or pine cones tied to the napkins . . . as in Contemporary Drama, South Region, and Northwest Region.
- Napkins and napkin rings can take on the role of individual centerpieces, depending on how they are arranged. The firecracker napkin ring arrangement is a good example of this . . . as in Flag-Waving Festival.

Firecracker Napkin Ring Arrangement

... as in Flag-Waving Festival

Cut narrow cardboard tubes (from wrapping paper rolls and so on) into 6-inch lengths and spray with red paint. Open a white fabric or paper napkin. Pinch the center of the napkin, and shake, letting the points fall down together, and tuck the pinched center down into the top of the tube. The napkin will look like the exploded end of a firecracker. Tuck several red and blue curly ribbon strands around the napkin, and let the ribbon ends fall freely. Set upright to the left of each place setting.

- Fancy folded napkins on the table or tucked into glassware will be sure to attract attention. These eye-catching napkin sculptures like the Cactus Fold and Mexican Fan Fold will put your wedding table on the best-dressed list . . . as in Southwest Region and Fanfare.

Cactus Fold

... as in Southwest Region

Use fabric or paper square napkins. Fold the square napkin into a smaller square, as if you were going to put it away in the linen closet. Fold this square into a triangle. Fold the triangle in half, with the open edges on the outside. Pleat, making the pleats about the size of the glass or napkin ring you will be using. Pinch the bottom of the pleated napkin with your thumb and finger. This is the base of the fold. Now, pull a single point down and a little below the base. Then take the second point and pull it down but not as far as the first point. Do the same for the third point. Leave the last point upright. Tuck into a glass or a napkin ring.

Mexican Fan Fold

... as in Fanfare

Use a fabric or paper napkin at least 15 inches square. Fold the napkin in half. Starting at one end of the rectangle, fold, accordion-style three-fourths of the length. The pleats can be as large or small as you wish to make them. One-half inch to 1 inch is the recommended width. Fold the napkin together lengthwise. There are two important points to remember about this napkin fold. First, fold the rectangular shape the long way with the pleats on the outside, and second, make sure the edges of the napkin are on top or farthest away from you. Now fold all the top corners of the unpleated section down to the opposite point next to the pleat to make a triangle. This will be the stand for your napkin fan. Finger-press this new fold line tightly, especially if you are using paper. Paper napkins have a tendency to fall apart unless this is folded tightly. Now be brave and set the fold on the table. Let go of the pleat and then let go of the fan. If you are using a paper napkin, turn the spine of the stand far to the left (if you are facing the back of the fold) to make sure the fan holds together.

Napkin Folding Book Source
. . . as in Banquet Room

Brighton Publications, Inc., P.O. Box 120706, St Paul, MN 55112-0706, (612)636-2220.

- For that gift box look, cover the tables with white tablecloths, and stretch 3-inch-wide ribbon end to end, both length and width of the table. Complete the gift box look with a big bow in the center. Arrange shiny, glass ball ornaments in and about the bow and sprinkle glitter on everything. Set candles close by so that the glass balls and glitter will reflect the candle flame, doubling the reflection value. Finish off with gold metallic gift cards at each place setting to serve as place cards . . . as in Mistletoe & Poinsettia.
- Use unexpected utensil holders or serving pieces such as terra cotta planters. You can find interesting pieces in garden centers . . . as in Southwest Region.
- Decorate champagne or sparkling water bottles with ribbons and balloons . . . as in Balloon Bash.

- Use ice coolers to hold flowers or champagne and sparkling water bottles . . . as in The Great Gatsby.

Ice Coolers

. . . as in The Great Gatsby

You'll need a round or square gallon container, paper or plastic, a half-gallon milk carton, distilled water, flower blossoms, uncooked rice, popcorn, or sand to weight a half-gallon carton, and waxed paper. You'll find gallon containers at a delicatessen.

Pour 1 inch of distilled water into the large container; freeze overnight. Place the milk carton on top of the ice in the center of the large container. Weight it down with rice, popcorn, or sand. Pour distilled water into the large container, almost to the top. Tuck in rosebuds, chrysanthemums, or any other kind of flower that is fairly large. Try to position the flowers so they don't bob to the surface. Then crumple a sheet of waxed paper and place it between the two containers, above the water. Do this on all four sides. This will keep the milk carton in the center. Be careful, when you wedge the waxed paper between the containers, that the paper doesn't touch the water; otherwise, the paper will freeze in the water. After the water has frozen solid, remove the waxed paper and pour out the weight material. Rock the milk carton back and forth until you can lift it out of the ice. To remove the outer container, let hot water run over the container for a second. Set the ice cooler in a bowl or on a cloth-covered tray. Place champagne bottle or flowers in the center.

- Dress the chairs as well as the table. Attach ribbons, bows, balloons, or small bouquets . . . as in Victorian Delight.

17. Favor Guide

F avor your guests with tokens of your appreciation. Although take-home gifts are just beginning to be favored here, party favors have long been a tradition in other countries. You'll appreciate how party favors can perk up each place setting or become an integral part of your wedding theme activity.

- Jordan almonds are usually offered as wedding favors, often in net bags. But they can also be tied in pinked, fabric squares to match the tablecloths or in a color or print to remind one of one's heritage . . . as in Poolside, Ethnic Food, and Table Setting.
- On the other hand, you can take a different approach and place candy instead of Jordan almonds in the traditional net bags. Try colorful mints or licorice candy pieces, in white netting . . . as in Balloon Bash and Contemporary Drama.
- Candies as favors can be given a little oomph simply by being packaged in a creative way. For instance, fill the tops of miniature parasols with mints, tuck lollipops into folded napkins, or pour jelly beans into plastic champagne glasses and add a straw . . . as in Parasol Style, Hearts & Flowers, and Easter Celebration.
- Candy favors can take unusual shapes, as well. You'll find long-stemmed chocolate roses and seashell-shaped truffles in candy stores. Or, make the Wedding Ring Kisses recipe (See the Decorative Recipe Guide.), and pop a tiny wedding charm on the tip before the candy hardens . . . as in The Great Gatsby, Gift from the Sea, and Casual Chic.

od memories grow? Favor your guests with growing
mind them of your wedding. Guests will enjoy receiv-
of garden seeds or small potted plants . . . as in
Spring Is Here and Southwest Region.

- Most anything will do for a favor if it's done well and given in the right setting. Some unusual favor ideas that work well are Christmas tree decorations, calendars printed in your ethnic language, and small packets of Fourth of July sparklers . . . as in Mistletoe & Poinsettia, Ethnic Food and Table Setting, and Flag-Waving Festival.
- Flowers, always a favorite gift, will be sure to make a colorful impression on your guests. Consider hibiscus hairpins or lapel flowers, fresh flower or paper leis, or one perfect rosebud trimmed with picot ribbon . . . as in Jamaica Bound, Hawaiian Luau, and Victorian Delight.
- Fragrant favors of scented potpourri or scented pine cones for coffee table or fireplace make a lasting and aromatic impression . . . as in Summer Time and Northwest Region.
- Tiny boxes of candy make elegant wedding favors. Tuck pieces of saltwater taffy in clear plastic boxes to show off the variety of colors. Pack marzipan candy in small white boxes or pen your initials and wedding date on gold boxes filled with liquor-filled truffles . . . as in Northeast Region, South Region, and Evening Formal.
- Just for fun, tie a balloon to each candy-filled box or bag, or tuck candies into a toy plastic convertible and wrap up with a length of netting . . . as in Balloon Bash and Fabulous Fifties.
- Lollipop favors are easy to find and can be seasonally or color coordinated to your wedding . . . as in Hearts & Flowers and Double Wedding.
- A clever rhyme or tender note attached to each favor adds an extra touch to wedding favors. Simply tuck a printed rhyme in a small truffle box or take a look at A Spoonful of Kisses and Sweet Pea Seed Favors . . . as in Informal Day and Puck's Perfect Party.

A Spoonful of Kisses

. . . .

Wrap three chocolate kisses in a plastic soup spo
ting to match your table colors. Tie a matching ri
loose ends of the netting and the handle of the spoon. Before tying,
run one end of the ribbon through a paper bell, saying: "A spoonful
of kisses brings lots of good wishes."

Sweet Pea Seed Favors

. . . as in Puck's Perfect Party

Purchase small packets of sweet pea seeds. Attach a paper note
(Pink the edges with a pinking shears.) to each seed packet, saying:
"Thank you for favoring us with your presence at our celebration.
Plant these seeds for their sweet fragrance and as a memory of this
occasion."

- Then, too, favoring your guests can be joined with an activity. For
  example, guests can have fun breaking a pinata and retrieving the
  fallen favors. Or, favor giving can take the form of a dramatic
  reenactment, such as gold chocolate coins given as a medieval tax
  forgiveness . . . as in Old Mexico and Medieval "Marry" Making.
- Candles make great giftables. Color-coordinated ribbon bows lift
  ordinary candles into the fancy favor category. And, a three-
  dimensional turkey candle is always good for a gobble during the
  Thanksgiving season . . . as in Light up the Night and Giving
  Thanks.
- Good favors can be better with some personalization. If both
  your names start with "M", offer M & M candies in net bags.
  Decorate truffles with your initials using frosting or print your
  names and wedding date on the favor. This works successfully on
  paper fans, flamingos and shells, or flowerpots . . . as in Fanfare,
  Key Largo, and Southwest Region.
- Find smooth rocks, about the size that will fit in the palm of your
  hand, and paint them in country colors. These paperweight

favors can then be decorated and inscribed with the message "Think Happy," along with your names and the date of your wedding . . . as in I Love Country.

- Lollipop favors are easy to find and can be seasonally or color coordinated to your wedding . . . as in Hearts & Flowers and Double Wedding.

Double Lollipop Favor

. . . as in Double Wedding

Find lollipops that reflect each bride's color choice. Sometimes you can find the kind that has a flower in the center of the lollipop. Cross the stick ends of two of the lollipops and tie securely with curly ribbon. Curl the ends of the ribbon and glue a small paper heart on each end. Small heart stickers can be used, too. Before the hearts are glued to the ribbon, write one couple's names on one heart and the other couple's names on the second heart.

- Box up an ethnic taste treat or bag a bagel for your guests' morning after . . . as in Ethnic Food and Table Setting and New York, New York!
- The boxed groom's cake, another tradition regarded as a favor for guests, is always popular. Choose from a variety of cakes, such as carrot cake, chocolate cake, or fruitcake . . . as in South Region.
- Baskets can hold tasty favor treats. Fillings for basket favors include stenciled miniature loaves of bread (See Stenciled Bread, Decorative Recipe Guide.) with preserves or an arrangement of fresh fruit . . . as in Midwest Region and Romantic Renaissance.

Wedding
18. Cake
Guide

After the bride, wedding cakes are most often "oohed" and "aahed" about. Although the traditional white layer cake still is the favorite, here and there you'll notice different-flavored cakes grabbing the spotlight. The best advice you can follow when ordering a wedding cake is to trust your own taste and order the kind of cake you like best.

- The lavish wedding cake has alternate layers of strawberry and chocolate cake and is decorated with off-white lattice-work frosting. Ivy is arranged between the tiered layers, and fresh flowers top the cake. Smaller flower-basket-shaped cakes decorated with sweet pea and rose flowers of spun sugar are placed at each side of the layer cake . . . as in Banquet Room.
- Contemporary wedding cakes are often made up of alternate layers of chocolate and white cake or simply an all-chocolate cake with white frosting. Fresh white flowers and green ivy trim the cake . . . as in Contemporary Drama.
- Complement a tropical theme with a key lime cake or a white cake with key lime filling, accented with twists of fresh lime and flowers . . . as in Key Largo.
- Substitute a pineapple upside-down cake for white cake. Offer alternative tropical desserts such as kiwi pie or banana cake . . . as in Jamaica Bound.
- Hot weather taste buds will enjoy a cake with raspberry mousse filling—moist, light, and delicious . . . as in Summer Time.

- For fall weddings, accent each cake layer and the top with fresh mums. Scatter autumn leaves at the base of the cake. A spice cake instead of the traditional white cake would be an unexpected seasonal taste treat . . . as in Autumn Harvest.
- Spring calls for a cake decorated with daisies instead of roses and a cluster of daisies as the cake topper. Wind a garland of daisies around the base of the cake . . . as in Spring Is Here.
- A wedding cake can stand a heavy dose of romantic symbolism. Select a heart-shaped cake decorated with pink hearts made of icing. Perch two Cupids on top of the cake . . . as in Hearts & Flowers.
- A specific theme is enhanced with the selection of just the right cake topper—for example, a miniature wedding couple under a parasol as a cake topper for a parasol theme . . . as in Parasol Style.
- Personalize your cake with a cake topper depicting your favorite sport or hobby . . . as in Northwest Region.
- Top your cake with your initials. Form a flexible wire into your initials and wind silk ivy leaves and white satin ribbon around the form. Or, simply ask your bakery to make initials of spun sugar for your cake topper . . . as in Formal Evening.
- If your layer cake has pillars between the layers, be sure to decorate the space in between. Fresh ivy or something like it can be very eye pleasing . . . as in Romantic Renaissance.
- Decorate the base of the cake with a circle of grapevine, ivy trimmed with ribbon, or a garland of daisies . . . as in Puck's Perfect Party, Romantic Renaissance, and Spring Is Here.
- Let your wedding cake represent your heritage. Some delicious possibilities are an Austrian, *Sacher Torte*, a chocolate cake served with whipped cream, a French, *Choux à la Crème*, a pyramid of small puff pastries filled with cream, or a Scandinavian, *Kronsekage*, a series of flat, round, ring cakes stacked to form a pyramid . . . as in Ethnic Wedding Customs.
- Two cakes, one for each bride, is sure to make a double impact . . . as in Double Wedding.

Decorative
Recipe
19. Guide

T hese tasty ideas are decorative as well as good to eat and drink. You can make the bread and cookies yourself or buy them at your local bakery if time is short. Either way, everyone will enjoy these tasteful and visual treats.

Stenciled Bread

. . . as in Midwest Region

Miniature bread loaves
Egg yolk
Red food coloring
Stencil brush
Heart stencil (small)

1. Bake or purchase miniature loaves of bread. It's best to give the bakery plenty of time for a special order like this.
2. Cool fresh baked bread.
3. Stir small amount of red food coloring into beaten egg yolk.
4. Place heart stencil on top of loaf and dab paint on the bread with a clean stencil brush. Let dry.

Wedding Kisses

... as in Casual Chic

4 cups sugar
1 cup light corn syrup
3/4 cup water
3 egg whites, stiffly beaten
1 teaspoon vanilla
1 cup chopped nuts
Decorative wedding rings (find them at wedding or party supply stores)

1. Place sugar, corn syrup, and water in a pan and heat. Stir until sugar dissolves. Cook, without stirring, to 255° F. A little of the mixture dropped into cold water will form a hard ball.
2. Remove from heat and pour, beating constantly, in a fine stream into the egg whites.
3. Continue beating until mixture holds its shape and loses its gloss.
4. Add the vanilla and nuts and stir.
5. Drop quickly from a spoon onto waxed paper, finishing in peaks.
6. Before candy hardens, place two wedding rings around the peak of each piece.
7. Makes about eight dozen pieces. (If you make this amount, ask a friend to help. Otherwise, the candy may harden before you put the rings on each piece.)

Cupid Cookies

... as in Hearts & Flowers

Sugar cookies (your favorite recipe or order from a bakery)
Pink decorator icing (see instructions)
Small round decorating tip
Gold wrapping string

1. If you bake, you'll need a Cupid cookie cutter. Otherwise, give the bakery plenty of time for this special order.

2. To make decorator icing, combine confec
   small amount of water, just enough to mak
   through a decorating tube yet hold its shape.
   of red food coloring.
3. With a small round decorating tip, outline a
   cooled cookie. Fill in with more pink icing. Le. harden.
4. Tie a gold string around Cupid's neck and finish off with a bow.

Lavender Punch

. . . as in Scenic Site

2 cups sugar
3 envelopes unsweetened grape drink mix
6 1/2 cups water
1 44-ounce jar pineapple-grapefruit juice
1/4 to 1/2 cup lemon juice
1 quart 7-Up
1 quart grape sherbet
Mix ingredients together. Makes about 40 servings. To change color of punch, use a different flavor of soft drink mix and flavor of sherbet.

Love Potion Number Nine Punch

. . . as in Hearts & Flowers

1 46-ounce can Pink Hawaiian Punch
1 44-ounce can pineapple-orange juice
1 12-ounce can frozen pink lemonade
2 quarts ginger ale
Mix together and add heart-shaped ice cubes.
Makes about 40 servings.

Decorations 20. for the Reception Guide

D ecorations can be as elaborate or as simple as you wish to
make them. Whatever the choice, these decorative ideas will
add a "Let's Celebrate" ambience to your reception. You're sure to
find an idea or two that will fit in nicely with your wedding plans.

- Decorate your reception area with good use of plants and flowers. Rented 8-foot ficus trees, trimmed with white lights, will
  minimize the starkness of a long hall. Set off entryways with ropes
  of fresh flowers and greens . . . as in Banquet Room.
- Use garlands of pine roping and gold metallic bows along the
  arches and entryways of the reception area. Add strings of tiny
  white lights . . . as in Northwest Region.
- Fill in empty reception areas with baskets of large paper flowers.
  You can find paper flowers in import shops or make them yourself.
  Pinatas and paper chains are good fillers, too . . . as in Old Mexico.
- Rent or purchase blooming bougainvillea and hibiscus plants to
  add color to the area. Traditional Southwest nonfloral accents
  include tin lampshades, bleached cattle skulls, and Indian pottery . . . as in Southwest Region.
- Masses of paper streamers, bows, hearts, and bells deliver a gala
  celebration message . . . as in Fabulous Fifties and Hearts &
  'rs.

forget to place a fresh bouquet of flowers in the women's
' room. It's the little things that are noticed . . . as in
' Room.

- Stains or cracks in the wall? Bring in rental pictures. Sneaky but effective . . . as in At Home.
- Commandeer travel posters, brochures, and calendars, whether of distant lands or Broadway theater, and use them for wall decorations . . . as in Hawaiian Luau and New York, New York!
- Set up a white lattice screen, wrapped with live or silk ivy. This will fill in empty areas, serve as a garden setting for photographs, and form a lovely backdrop for the cake cutting ceremony . . . as in Summer Time.
- A beautiful ice sculpture will collect its share of "oohs" and "aahs." Choose a flower basket form and fill the basket with fresh seasonal flowers. If management can't provide the ice sculpture, try your nearest vocational school . . . as in Banquet Room.
- Create a fantasy garden setting with a water fountain . . . as in Winter Garden.
- Add romantic light to the setting with luminarias, tiki torches, or Japanese lanterns . . . as in Light up the Night, Hawaiian Luau, and Poolside.
- Prop or stand a decorative lace or honeycomb parasol on the gift table. To stand, pop the parasol handle into an shiny paper designer bag and fill with light sand or birdseed. Loosely wrap the top of the bag around the handle with a ribbon and bow. Decorate the handle with flowers and twine narrow ribbons from the top, letting the ribbons fall naturally . . . as in Parasol Style.
- A quilt with squares contributed by friends and relatives and put together by you adds a personal decorative touch to your reception. Hang on the wall behind the head table or drape it across the guest book table . . . as in I Love Country.
- Run drapery roping in loops along the skirt sides of the tables. Cluster fresh ivy at the top of each loop, letting some of the longer ivy strands drop down almost to the floor. Before arranging, condition the ivy by soaking leaves and all in cool water . . . as in Romantic Renaissance.
- Casual collections can sometimes add the crowning touch to a decorating scene. Dig out a collection of fancy broaches or but-

tons, fans, or seashells and use them as focal points on fancy table swags . . . as in Key Largo.

- Old family wedding pictures are fun to look at and can be a real decorative plus. Set the pictures on the guest book table or blow them up to poster size and hang them on the wall . . . as in Reaffirmation and Sentimental Reasons.
- Plush animals lend a whimsical look to the reception. Set a pair of Christmas mice, Thanksgiving geese, or Easter bunnies, all dressed in wedding regalia, in prominent spots. Rent a life-size plush rabbit and set prominently at the reception entrance to greet your guests. Hang an Easter basket filled with Easter egg favors or net rice bags on the rabbit's arm . . . as in Easter Celebration.
- Weddings during the holiday season benefit from seasonal decorations already in place. For example, mistletoe, poinsettia, and Christmas trees add to the celebration spirit . . . as in Mistletoe & Poinsettia.
- Balloons signal a gala event, as they will for your reception . . . as in Balloon Bash.

Balloon Tips

. . . as in Balloon Bash

Any number of good companies out there will fill your wedding world with balloons. But, if you think you can round up a balloon committee, you may want to try decorating your wedding yourself.

You should know that there are two kinds of balloons; latex (rubber) and mylar. Latex comes in many colors and is easy to personalize with special artwork or printing. Flying time is 12 to 14 hours if you buy quality balloons. Helium tanks can be rented very reasonably at any rental store.

Mylar balloons are becoming very popular because they hold helium longer, at least three to four days. It's been said that some mylar balloons will last up to three years. In that case, the wedding couple could save a few balloons and use them on their first anniversary. It's worth a try.

- Give top billing to your wedding by renting a billboard that you can light up with your names, much like a theater marquee. More theater impact can come from colored light bulbs, white lights, and spotlights . . . as in New York, New York!
- A rental tent is practically a must at an outdoor wedding. Tents conveniently come in many colors and sizes. To decorate, wind garlands of myrtle, asparagus ferns, and tiny white lights around the supporting poles of the tent. Fix oasis cages of fern fronds to the bottom of the poles and around the stakes. Set pots of blooming flowers around for color . . . as in Lawn and Garden.
- If your reception is held in a pool area, decorate the pool. Nestle plastic containers of flowers inside childrens' water safety rings. Tie bunches of balloons, filled with helium, to the rings. Check your pool supply store for ways to anchor the rings, or let them float freely. Set floating candles in the water to light up the evening . . . as in Poolside.
- Contrary to popular opinion, nature can be improved upon. One way is to tie satin ribbon bows to the trees outlining your ceremony or reception area . . . as in Scenic Setting.
- When you have big crowds in a limited space, forget the formal centerpieces. They're space wasters. Arrange flowers in small baskets or bud vases instead . . . as in At Home.
- Rent the surroundings that give you the atmosphere you love. For period themes, rent a historical mansion, inn, or restaurant . . . as in The Great Gatsby and Northeast Region.
- Include the service people in your overall decoration plans. Dress them in theme costumes. It can be as simple as everyone wearing matching T-shirts or as elaborate as wearing period costumes . . . as in Poolside and Northeast Region.
- Believe it or not, what you and your guests wear does have a decorative effect on your wedding. Summery, light dress for garden weddings, informal dress for scenic site weddings, or black or white formal wear only, for guests and wedding party is important . . . as in Contemporary Drama.

Decorations
for the
Ceremony
Guide 21.

N ever forgetting that the wedding ceremony is a serious occasion, express some of the joy you feel with decorations. A potted plant, a few candles, or an array of ribbon bows may be all you need. Remember, too, that some of the decorations from the wedding may be moved and used in the reception area.

- Set tubs of flowers, greenery, flowering bulbs, or clusters of balloons in the sanctuary area. Everything can be transferred to the reception and the plants can be saved and replanted later . . . as in Winter Garden, Southwest Region, and Balloon Bash.
- Decorate with arches of balloons across every fourth row of seats. Attach the balloon arches to the pews with white satin bows. White, silver, or confetti-filled balloons are usually used for weddings. Sometimes you can find clear balloons filled with smaller balloons. The smaller balloons inside can be in your wedding colors. Since balloon arches are a bit tricky, you may need the help of balloon professionals for this decorating step . . . as in Balloon Bash.
- Mark the guest pews by attaching ribbon and lace bows . . . as in Victorian Delight.

Step-by-Step Bowmaking

. . . as in Victorian Delight

Start with a 1-inch loop, being careful to position the loop far enough up the ribbon to leave enough at the end for a ribbon streamer. This 1-inch loop will be the center loop. Pinch the loop together (the underpart of the loop) with your thumb and forefinger. Then twist the ribbon (between loop and ribbon reel but at a point close to loop) so shiny side is up. Make a loop on one side of the center loop. Twist (because you want the shiny side of ribbon up) and pinch. Then make a loop on the other side of the center loop. Make three to five loops on each side of center loop. To hold together, use taped wire. Because pew bows look better with extra streamers, attach a separate length of ribbon at the center to the underside of the center loop. Pinch, to wire bow and streamers together. Make the streamers at least 2 feet long, so they will be long enough to move with the air currents.

Attaching Pew Markers

Cut a short piece of 2-to 3-inch carpet tape. Tape the wire to the pew. Keep the tape piece long enough to hold, but short enough so it will be covered by the bow, flower, or other pew marker.

- Instead of bows, attach fans trimmed with a fresh flower to the pews. At some craft stores, you can find fans that have florist foam already attached . . . as in Fanfare.
- To achieve a fresh springtime look, hang a personalized windsock near the altar and tuck a pinwheel through the knot of each ribbon and bow pew marker . . . as in Spring Is Here.
- A spray of dried grasses, strands of ivy, a mini-bouquet of fall leaves, or a sprig of evergreen trimmed with ribbon create simple but lovely pew markers . . . as in Midwest Region, South Region, Autumn Harvest, and Northwest Region.
- Greet your guests with reed half-baskets of ivy attached to the doors leading to your ceremony . . . as in South Region.

- Decorate the candleholders and candles with ribbon and bows . . . as in Light up the Night.
- In some cases, churches or temples have pew tapers you can use during the ceremony . . . as in Light up the Night.
- The unity candle is decorative as well as symbolic of the sharing of a lifetime together. Sometime during the ceremony, the bride and groom light the candle simultaneously . . . as in Light up the Night.

Music
Guide
22.

Music and weddings go together like love and marriage, but sometimes it's hard to know what music is the right music for your wedding. A good approach is to choose music for the ceremony that is meaningful to you. Later, at the reception, you'll want dinner and dance music that will be enjoyed by everyone.

- For sentimental value, use a selection of music from your parents' wedding for your ceremony. Or, select a piece that has played a part in your courtship days . . . as in Sentimental Reasons.
- Introduce ethnic music into the recessional wedding march. Bagpipes or drums, with their rhythmic beat, are two instruments that lend themselves well to an ethnic-flavored recessional. Find ethnic music at your local library, music societies, or local cultural organizations . . . as in Ethnic Ceremony.
- Liturgical dancing performed to the strains of a ballad or folk song from your heritage is a fitting highlight to the ceremony . . . as in Ethnic Ceremony.
- The sound of birds singing at an outdoor wedding may not be the same as an organ, but the music is still wonderful in its own way . . . as in Scenic Setting.

- Taped music for the ceremony and reception is a space saver for the at-home wedding . . . as in At Home.
- Country-style entertainment like fiddle or banjo music will start feet tapping to its special beat . . . as in I Love Country.
- Softly playing chimes, harp, or woodwind quartet exudes magical notes of enchantment . . . as in Puck's Perfect Party.
- The gentle music of the mandolin or lute will give you a medieval or renaissance romantic sound . . . as in Medieval "Marry" Making.
- Dance your first wedding dance to romantic music or love songs meaningful to you. "My Funny Valentine" is especially appropriate for a Valentine wedding . . . as in Hearts & Flowers.

23. Floral Bouquet Guide

B ouquets are a lovely and integral part of any wedding ceremony. Traditionally, an abundance of flowers symbolized a life of plenty for the wedding couple. Today, selecting bouquets is much like choosing the fashions you wear . . . you pick whatever suits you. You'll find lovely ideas for floral bouquets and some interesting alternatives in the following suggestions.

- Fresh flower circlets in the hair and grapevine wreaths carried casually in one hand take the place of traditional floral bouquets . . . as in Puck's Perfect Party.
- Pearl sprays (pearls strung on a monofilament strand) make graceful fill-ins for bouquets . . . as in Gifts from the Sea.
- Have a strand of heirloom pearls or other heirloom pieces ? Ask your florist to design your bridal bouquet incorporating the jewelry . . . as in Gifts from the Sea.
- Dress up a hand-held fan with flowers and ribbons for an unusual wedding bouquet treatment . . . as in Fanfare.
- Add a little flower power to parasols that are carried in place of bouquets. Drape 8-inch-wide lengths of ribbon from the top of the parasol and add small flowers to the ribbons with love knots . . . as in Parasol Style.
- Freesia, lily of the valley, stephanotis, Queen Anne's lace, and roses are popular choices for an all-white traditional bridal bouquet. White calla lilies and dendrobium lend a sophisticated

look to bridal bouquets . . . as in Traditionally Yours and New York, New York!

- Duplicate your mother's wedding bouquet with the help of old wedding photographs . . . as in Sentimental Reasons.
- Blend several sentimental thoughts into one bouquet. For example, tuck your grandmother's lace handkerchief into a bouquet of pink roses, the kind given to you on your first date . . . as in Sentimental Reasons.
- A rounded cluster of flowers backed with a lace holder typifies the country look . . . as in I Love Country.
- Bridesmaids carry all-white cascade bouquets in sharp contrast to their elegant black dresses . . . as in Contemporary Drama.
- Tiny net or lace bags of potpourri can be tied to the ribbon streamers of a tight cluster of flowers . . . as in the Northeast Region and South Region.
- Explore Grandmother's button box for old lace pieces to tuck into a cluster bouquet of roses. Either roll the lace into rosebuds or use strips of lace in place of ribbon streamers . . . as in Victorian Delight.

Lace Rosebuds

. . . as in Victorian Delight

You will need a strip of lace about 8 inches long by 2 or 3 inches wide, florist tape, and thin florist wire. Fold over the end of the lace about 1 inch. Fold again. Place the tip of florist wire into the center of the fold. Fold the lace around the fold and wire, wrapping the lower edge tighter than the top edge. Continue winding the lower edge of the lace tightly around the fold and wire, letting the lace edge drop just a little lower each time it goes around. Wrap florist tape around the lower edge of the lace bud and down on the wire.

- For an authentic fifties look, carry a white crescent-shaped bouquet or a dainty round nosegay. The bridesmaids carry a smaller version of the bridal bouquet featuring pink and white carnations. The men in the wedding party can tuck a pink rosebud or carnation into their lapel . . . as in Fabulous Fifties.

- A backing of cluny lace adds a touch of romance to the nosegay. Cluny comes in white or ivory, in a 6-, 8-, or10-inch round backing. It can be spray-painted a matching color . . . as in Spring Is Here.

- Don't dismiss silk floral bouquets. Besides being a lovely keepsake, they seem to have been designed especially for the winter bride . . . as in Winter Garden.

- Look to major holidays to inspire creative bouquets. Easter baskets, patriotic colors, harvesttime flowers, and holiday jingle bells all enjoy the wedding bouquet spotlight . . . as in Easter Celebration, Flag-Waving Festival, Giving Thanks, and Mistletoe & Poinsettia.

- Pride in your past will be beautifully obvious if your bouquets display well-known colors, flowers, or accessories from your heritage . . . as in Ethnic Dress.

- Exotic floral bouquets signal a tropical mood. Choose sweet-scented orchids, plumeria, tuberose, hibiscus, or bougainvillea and arrange them in a loose, casual bouquet. A sprig or one blossom of these flowers serves well as a lapel flower, too . . . as in Hawaiian Luau and Jamaica Bound.

- Gather bouquets of strawflowers, daisies, zinnias, and bee balm in assorted hot-salsa colors. Garnish with brightly striped grosgrain ribbons . . . as in Old Mexico.

- Use an unusual focal point such as seashells in a cascade-style bouquet. Then fill in with any of your favorite in-season flowers . . . as in Key Largo

- When you choose flowers in season, you're more likely to stay within your budget. Every season offers a bounteous bouquet . . . as in Spring Is Here, Summer Time, Autumn Harvest, and Winter Garden.

- Carry a simple nosegay or a single stemmed flower, or wear a corsage for the informal wedding . . . as in Informal Day.

- In a civil ceremony, the bride's flowers take their cue from the style of dress. A corsage or small bouquet is appropriate even if the ceremony is held in the county clerk's office . . . as in Civil Ceremony.
- When bridesmaids wear different dress styles and colors, the best way to achieve a cohesive wedding party look is to purchase similar bouquets for you and them . . . as in Reaffirmation.

24.
Fashion
Guide

For most people, shopping for dresses is the highlight of preparations for a wedding. Since choosing the wedding attire is such a personal matter, the following are suggestions only to help you arrive at the best solution.

- When you are shopping for dresses, shop for the season when the wedding is to be held. Don't buy heavy winter dresses for a July wedding date . . . as in Summer Time.
- Shoes are an important consideration, too. Choose shoes appropriate to the location . . . as in Lawn and Garden.
- Before making a decision on the length of train or whether to have a train at all, try to visualize your activity during the wedding: walking on grass, dancing, and so on . . . as in Lawn and Garden.
- A suit or street length dress for the bride and a suit for the groom are perfectly appropriate for certain kinds of ceremonies . . . as in Informal Day and Civil Ceremony.
- A formal wedding dictates formal attire for the entire wedding party . . . as in Formal Evening.
- A white wedding dress symbolizes joy and can be worn for any type of wedding . . . as in Second Marriage.
- Accessories like crocheted gloves, parasols, and pearl jewelry can emphasize a chosen wedding theme . . . as in I Love Country, Parasol Style, and Gifts from the Sea.

- Draw color and style inspiration from your theme. Choose holiday-inspired fashion like nautical-styled dresses with straw hats as a nod to the Fourth of July, or borrow a color scheme from the region or season . . . as in Flag-waving Festival, Midwest Region, or Giving Thanks.
- Restyle or design a copy of your mother's wedding dress, creating a special bond . . . as in Sentimental Reasons.
- Clothing and accessories chosen from your ethnic background make a positive statement about your heritage . . . as in Ethnic Dress.
- Historical themes are enhanced with authentic dress of the time . . . as in Medieval "Marry" Making, Romantic Renaissance, Victorian Delight, and Fabulous Fifties.

Historical Dress Pattern Sources
. . . as in Medieval "Marry" Making
and Victorian Delight

Amazon Drygoods, 2218 E 11th St., Davenport, IA 52803, (319) 322-6800.
Past Patterns, 217 S 5th St., Richmond, IN 47374, (317) 962-3333

- You can make sure you and your bridesmaids have a one-of-a-kind dress by handpainting flowers on the fabric. Personalize the dresses by painting the birthday flower of each bridesmaid on her dress . . . as in Casual Chic.

Fabric Painting Hints
. . . as in Casual Chic

1. Designs can be airbrushed or stenciled.
2. The heavier the fabric, the less the paint will disturb the flow of the fabric.
3. Airbrushing gives a soft muted look. Colors blend easily.
4. Stenciling leaves solid definition between colors.
5. You can buy stencil patterns at any hobby shop.

6. Paints have to be heat set. This is usually done with a hot iron. It's important, then, to get a fabric that will withstand the heat needed to set the paint.
7. Dyes do not have to be heated, but pigments do.
8. Cut fabric into pattern pieces before you stencil. Sew the pieces together after you paint.
9. Plan your design so it does not go into the seam line. Figure for the seam allowance.
10. An overskirt of sheer material over handpaint fabric will create a misty-looking print.
11. You will need a firm surface for stenciling. Use newspaper wrapped in clean white tissue paper on your table or other surface.
12. Cover the rest of the fabric when airbrushing to protect it from stray flecks of paint.

nory
ıvıaker
Guide 25.

E very couple, it seems, remembers their wedding day as a
blur of activities accompanied by a general sense of euphoria. For this reason, it's important to build into your wedding plans
at least one, if not several, memory makers, things that you can
look over during a quiet time or use at your anniversary celebrations to help you remember and enjoy again your day of days.

- The traditional memory keeper is the wedding guest book.
  Place the book in a prominent spot or ask some of the
  younger members of the family to take the book around to the
  guests for signing . . . as in South Region.
- The ribbon and lace used for bow pew markers can be reused
  later for remembrance pillows for sofa or bed . . . as in
  Victorian Delight.
- Quilts are America's treasured memory keepers. You can create an elegant and memorable quilt from your bridal and
  bridesmaid dress remnants. But the best kind of quilt is one
  whose handwork is shared by friends and relatives. Each person contributes a designed square that is meaningful for them
  and you. Then you piece the squares together before the wedding so everyone can enjoy the quilt on your wedding day . . .
  as in I Love Country.
- A signature tablecloth sets off the best of memories from your
  wedding. Drape a lace-edged tablecloth on the guest book

table. Keep a textile pen handy for your signatures. Later, work the signatures and the date of your wedding with embroidery floss . . . as in Casual Chic.

- Plenty of picture taking and video and audio recordings will keep factual records of this most important day . . . as in Sentimental Reasons.

- A special memory candle can be made to light up subsequent anniversaries. After the festivities, a friend or parent can collect the leftover candles. Then melt the stubs and make one large candle. Decorate with memorabilia like an imprinted paper napkin, invitation, or snapshot from the wedding . . . as in Light up the Night.

- Save any imprinted paper napkins. They can be used when you enjoy your intimate first anniversary picnic . . . as in Fabulous Fifties.

- Treasure your wedding dress. The day will come sooner than you can imagine when the next generation will want to wear it or have a copy of the design made. Or, wear it yourself at your 50th wedding anniversary . . . as in Sentimental Reasons.

- Some types of cake will keep well enough so that you can save the top layer (freeze it) and serve it on your first anniversary. Cakes with butter in the frosting may not keep as well but fruitcake and other types of cakes work well . . . as in Double Wedding, Traditionally Yours, Contemporary Drama, and Autumn Harvest.

- Your cake topper can represent your heritage and be a permanent reminder of your wedding day . . . as in Ethnic Wedding Customs.

- An everlasting bouquet placed under a glass bell can be enjoyed for a long time as can a second bouquet made for the purpose of a keepsake after the bouquet throwing ritual . . . as in Winter Garden and Fanfare.

26.
Younger Set
Guide

T he kids in your family can play meaningful roles in your wedding, too. As a matter of fact, you're going to be surprised at just how much they can add to the joyfulness of your wedding day. So give them a chance; their delighted smiles will be reward enough.

- Your flower girl will delight your guests, handing out daisies as she walks down the aisle ahead of you . . . as in Spring Is Here.
- Young children can precede you down the aisle, dropping scented flower petals . . . as in Second Marriage.
- If you let the kids in the crowd use inexpensive cameras or Polaroids, you'll be assured of a different kind of pictorial perspective of your wedding . . . as in Sentimental Reasons.
- Dress two or three young members of the family as medieval pages. Give them bags of gold coins (gold-foil-wrapped chocolate candy) to hand out as favors to the guests . . . as in Medieval "Marry" Making.
- Dress your child attendants in ethnic costumes to represent your heritage . . . as in Ethnic Dress.
- Younger members of the family can see to the clean cups, spoons, and condiments of a pre-ceremony hot beverage offering . . . as in Winter Garden Theme.

- Your children, if old enough, may want to formally announce the reaffirmation by their parents and extend an invitation to the ceremony . . . as in Reaffirmation.
- Some of the young set might volunteer to take the guest book around to the guests for signing . . . as in South Region.
- Older children can be your attendants and join together with friends and family in loving support of your marriage . . . as in Second Marriage.

27.
Rice-Throwing
Guide

T hrowing rice on the wedding day is a not-to-be-missed ritual. In the following ideas, the ritual is kept, but the rice is
replaced with some delightful substitutes. Perhaps some of these
ideas will inspire you to new rice-throwing heights.

- Throwing rice or birdseed at the newly marrieds bestows good
  luck on the guests and abundance on the newlyweds . . . as in
  Traditionally Yours.
- Instead of rice as a symbol of good wishes, release helium-
  filled balloons after the ceremony . . . as in Balloon Bash.
- Wrap confetti paper stars or tiny red foil hearts instead of rice
  into netting . . . as in Hearts & Flowers.
- When it's time for the rice-throwing fun, give everyone a small
  jar of soap bubbles trimmed with festive ribbon. Blowing
  bubbles will ensure a bountiful life—wet, but bountiful . . . as
  in Poolside.

Activity and Attractions
28. Guide

R eward your guests with special activities and attractions. Your guests have come to celebrate your marriage, so give them some stimulus and means to celebrate. Plan a wedding that's fun and exciting for yourself as well as for your guests.

- After-dinner dancing is a favorite wedding activity. Whether you engage a big dance band, a three-piece combo, or a disc jockey, after-dinner dancing is enjoyed by all. Match the music selection to your guest list . . . as in New York, New York!, Fabulous Fifties, Ethnic Wedding Customs, and Southwest Region.
- A folk dance show during intermission brightens the festivities. Better yet, dance lessons given by the troupe will have everyone participating in the folk dances . . . as in Ethnic Wedding Customs and Hawaiian Luau.
- Creative transportation here and there on the wedding day adds to the color and excitement of the day—not to mention great picture-taking opportunities. Enjoy horse-drawn carriage rides, dash off to wedding or reception sites in motor launches or horse-drawn sleighs, or parade in rented classic cars . . . as in Northeast Region, Northwest Region, and The Great Gatsby.
- For listening pleasure, enlist the aid of barbershop quartets or choral groups such as Merry England carolers . . . as in Mistletoe & Poinsettia.

- Employ mimes or local acting talent to plant themselves as "live" statues in the reception area, only to come alive at opportune moments . . . as in Medieval "Marry" Making.
- Everyone will get a kick out of watching the local dance line strut their stuff . . . as in New York, New York!
- Entertain with a homemade script lifted from a famous love scene. Local drama groups can help you. Insert your names and stories from your courtship days into the drama . . . as in Giving Thanks.
- Sparks will fly if you put on a fireworks spectacular for your guests . . . as in Flag-Waving Festival.
- A continuously run silent video, as a combination of entertainment and decorative background, can help set the theme's atmosphere for the day. Choose a romantic love story such as an old Humphrey Bogart movie . . . as in Key Largo.
- Balloon drops puts more "gala" into gala affairs. Rent shower nets and fill with balloons blown up with air instead of helium. Air-filled balloons will fall rather than rise when they are released . . . as in Balloon Bash.
- Pinatas are fun for everyone regardless of age . . . as in Old Mexico.
- Let your guests become the stars as they pose behind cartoonlike painted billboard scenes . . . as in Victorian Delight.
- Even a simple activity such as offering cups of hot chocolate, tea, or coffee before the ceremony to take the chill out of a cold day brings expressions of appreciation . . . as in Winter Garden.

Wedding
29. Toasts

The best man offers the toast to the bride or the bride and groom. Then, in some cases, the bridemaid will follow with a toast. The toast can be simple and from the heart or it can be a classic toast as is the Irish Toast.

—Irish Toast
May you be poor in misfortune,
Rich in blessings,
Slow to make enemies,
Quick to make friends.
But rich or poor, quick or slow
May you know nothing
but happiness
From this day forward.

—Toast I
To Maria and Tony:
We celebrate your love with this toast:
May your lives together be a continuation of the love, joy and togetherness we share today.

—Toast II

To Jane:
May the happiness of today give you pleasure in your tomorrows.

—Toast III

To Bill and Valerie:
May the joy of today continue,
May the love you share be your strength,
May your friendship carry you through good times and bad,
And may your lives be filled with the love of
friends, family and each other.

—Toast IV

To Jan and Brian:
Here's to good health, happiness, and a lifelong honeymoon.

Wedding
Plan
Pages

These wedding plan pages will lead you through a problem free wedding. Use as is or copy into a small spiral notebook.

First things First

Preferred Wedding _____

Guest List Estimate _____

Reception Site

    Place _____

    Date _____

    Time _____

    Telephone Number _____

    Confirmed _____

Caterer

    Name _____

    Telephone Number _____

    Confirmed _____

Ceremony

Place _____

Date _____

Time _____

Telephone Number _____

Confirmed _____

Wedding Dress

Store or Seamstress_____

Telephone Number _____

Fitting Date _____

Pickup Date _____

Bridesmaids' Dress

Store or Seamstress_____

Telephone Number _____

Fitting Date _____

Pickup Date _____

Photographer

Name _____

Telephone Number _____

Confirmed _____

Band or Disc Jockey

Name _____

Telephone Number _____

Confirmed _____

THREE MONTHS BEFORE THE WEDDING

Invitations

   Ordered from_____

   Pickup Date _____

Tuxedos

   Rental Name _____

   Telephone Number _____

   Confirmed _____

Florist

   Name _____

   Telephone Number _____

   Confirmed _____

Ceremony

   Musician _____

   Vocalist _____

Transportation for Wedding Party

   Name _____

   Telephone Number _____

   Confirmed _____

Audio or Video Recording

   Name _____

   Telephone Number _____

   Confirmed _____

FOUR WEEKS BEFORE THE WEDDING

Invitations

    Date Mailed _____

Wedding Reception Favors _____

Attendants' Gifts _____

Wedding Cake

    Name of Bakery _____

    Telephone Number _____

Guests' Overnight Arrangements

    Place _____

    Address _____

    Telephone Number _____

Guests' Transportation from Airport

    Service _____

    Date _____

    Time _____

Guest Parking

    Place _____

    Service _____

Final Dress Fitting

    Place _____

    Date _____

    Time _____

Purchase Wedding Guest Book _____

TWO WEEKS BEFORE THE WEDDING

Newspaper Forms for Wedding Announcements

Newspaper _____

Address _____

_____

Telephone Number _____

Pick Up Marriage License

Photography Session for the Wedding Party

Place _____

Date _____

Time _____

LAST WEEK

Pick Up Rental Equipment _____

Give Final Guest Count to the Caterer _____

Check Photo or Video Arrangements and Prepare a List of Must-Have Pictures _____

Check Florist Arrangements _____

Check Music Arrangements and Any Reception Activities _____

List Special Dances and Song Requests for the Band Leader or Disc Jockey _____

Check the Wedding Cake Delivery Arrangements _____

Prepare Emergency Kit (Stockings, Band-Aids, Combs) _____

Theme Index

At Home, 80
Autumn Harvest, 75

Balloon Bash, 19
Banquet Room, 78

Casual Chic, 27
Civil Ceremony, 92
Contemporary Drama, 33

Double Wedding, 90

Easter Celebration, 52
Ethnic Ceremony, 59
Ethnic Dress, 58
Ethnic Food and Table Setting, 61
Ethnic Wedding Customs, 62

Fabulous Fifties, 48
Fanfare, 22
Flag-Waving Festival, 53
Formal Evening, 87

Gifts from the Sea, 21
Giving Thanks, 54
Great Gatsby, The, 46

Hawaiian Luau, 64
Hearts & Flowers, 50

I Love Country, 30
Informal Day, 86

Jamaica Bound, 70

Key Largo, 68

Lawn and Garden, 81
Light up the Night, 25

Medieval "Marry" Making, 42
Midwest Region, 38
Mistletoe & Poinsettia, 56

New York, New York!, 67
Northeast Region, 35
Northwest Region, 39

Old Mexico, 65

Poolside, 83
Parasol Style, 23
Puck's Perfect Party, 18

Reaffirmation, 93
Romantic Renaissance, 43

Second Marriage, 89
Sentimental Reasons, 32
Scenic Setting, 84
South Region, 36
Southwest Region, 40
Spring Is Here, 72
Summer Time, 73

Traditionally Yours, 28

Victorian Delight, 45

Winter Garden, 76

General Index

A

Activity and Attractions, 143-144
Attaching Pew Markers
(decorations for the
ceremony),
instructions for, 127-128
Attendant Gifts, 99-100

B

Balloon Tips (decorations for
the reception), 124

C

Cactus Fold (table setting),
instructions for, 110
Centerpieces, 103-107
Della Robia Centerpiece,
instructions for, 104
Fireside Basket Centerpiece,
instructions for, 105
Gifts from the Sea Centerpiece,
instructions for, 102-103
Grapevine Wreath,
instructions for, 107
Patriotic Centerpiece,
instructions for, 105
Cupid Cookies
(decorative recipe),
instructions for, 120-121

D

Decorations for the Ceremony,
127-128
Attaching Pew Markers,
instructions for, 127-128

Step-by-Step Bowmaking,
instructions for, 127
Decorations for the Reception,
122-125
Balloon Tips, 124
Decorative Recipes, 119-121
Stenciled Bread,
instructions for, 119
Wedding Ring Kisses,
instructions for, 120
Cupid Cookies,
instructions for, 120-121
Lavender Punch,
instructions for, 121
Love Potion Number Nine,
instructions for, 121
"Decorative Themes," 18-26
Balloon Bash, 19-21
Fanfare, 22-23
Gifts from the Sea, 21-22
Light up the Night, 25-26
Parasol Style, 23-25
Puck's Perfect Party, 18-19
Della Robbia Centerpiece
(centerpiece),
instructions for, 104
"Destination Themes," 64-71
Hawaiian Luau, 64-65
Jamaica Bound, 70-71
Key Largo, 68-70
New York, New York!, 67-68
Old Mexico, 65-67
Double Lollipop Favor
(favor),
instruction for, 116

F

Fabric Painting Hints (fashion), hints for, 136-137

Fashion, 135-137
Fabric Painting Hints, hints for, 136-137
Historical Dress Pattern Sources, addresses, 136

Favors, 113-116
Double Lollipop Favor, instructions for, 116
Spoonful of Kisses, A, instructions for, 115
Sweet Pea Seed Favors, instructions for, 115-116
Wedding Ring Kisses, instructions for, 120

Firecracker Napkin Ring Arrangement (table setting), instructions for, 110

Fireside Basket Centerpiece (centerpiece), instructions for, 105

Floral Bouquets, 131-134
Lace Rosebuds, instructions for, 132

G

Gifts from the Sea Centerpiece (centerpiece), instructions for, 102-103

Grapevine Wreath (centerpiece), instructions for, 107

H

"Heritage Themes," 58-63
Ethnic Ceremony, 59-61
Ethnic Dress, 58-59
Ethnic Food and Table Setting, 61-62
Ethnic Wedding Customs, 62-63

Historical Dress Pattern Sources (fashion), addresses, 136

"Holiday Themes," 50-57
Easter Celebration, 52-53
Flag-Waving Festival, 53-54
Giving Thanks, 54-55
Hearts & Flowers, 50-51
Mistletoe & Poinsettia, 56-57

I

Ice Coolers (table setting), instructions for, 112

Invitations, 101-102

L

Lace Rosebuds (floral bouquet), instructions for, 132

Lavender Punch (decorative recipe), instructions for, 121

Love Potion Number Nine (decorative recipe), instructions for, 121

M

Memory Makers, 138-139

Mexican Fan Fold (table setting), instructions for, 110-111

Music, 129-130

N
Napkin Folding Book Source,
(table setting),
address, 111
Napkins, *See* Table Napkins,
instructions for folding.

P
Patriotic Centerpiece
(centerpiece),
instructions for, 105
Punch Recipes. *See* Decorative
Recipes.

R
"Regional Themes," 35-41
Midwest Region, 38-39
Northeast Region, 35-36
Northwest Region, 39-40
South Region, 36-37
Southwest Region, 40-41
Rice-Throwing, 142

S
"Seasonal Themes," 72-77
Autumn Harvest, 75-76
Spring Is Here, 72-73
Summer Time, 73-75
Winter Garden, 76-77
"Special Sites Themes," 78-85
At Home, 80-81
Banquet Room, 78-79
Lawn and Garden, 81-83
Poolside, 83-84
Scenic Setting, 84-85

Spoonful of Kisses Favor, A
(favor),
instructions for, 115
Stenciled Bread (decorative
recipe),
instructions for, 119
Step-By-Step Bowmaking
(decorations for the
ceremony),
instructions for, 127
"Style Setting Themes," 27-34
Casual Chic, 27-28
Contemporary Drama, 33-34
I Love Country, 30-31
Sentimental Reasons, 32-33
Traditionally Yours, 28-30
Sweet Pea Seed Favors (favor),
instructions for, 115-116

T
Table Napkin, instruction for
folding, 110-111
Cactus Fold, 110
Mexican Fan Fold, 110-111
Table Setting, 108-112
Cactus Fold,
instructions for, 110
Firecracker Napkin Ring
Arrangement,
instructions for, 110
Ice Coolers,
instructions for, 112
Mexican Fan Fold,
instructions for, 110-111
"Timeless Themes," 42-49
Fabulous Fifties, 48-49
Great Gatsby, The, 46-48

Medieval "Marry" Making,
    42-43
Romantic Renaissance, 43-45
Victorian Delight, 45-46
"Today's Ceremony Themes,"
    86-95
  Civil Ceremony, 92-93
  Double Wedding, 90-92
  Formal Evening, 87-89
  Informal Day, 86-87
  Reaffirmation, 93-95
  Second Marriage, 89-90

W
Wedding Cakes, 117-118
Wedding Plan Pages, 147-151
Wedding preparation checklist,
    96-98
Wedding Ring Kisses
    (decorative recipe),
    instructions for, 120
Wedding Toasts, 145-146

Y
Younger Set, The, 140-141

Available from Brighton Publications, Inc.

Wedding Hints & Reminders by Sharon Dlugosch

Wedding Occasions: 101 New Party Themes for Wedding Showers, Rehearsal Dinners, Engagement Parties, and More! by Cynthia Lueck Sowden

Dream Weddings Do Come True: How to Plan a Stress-free Wedding by Cynthia Kreuger

Games for Wedding Shower Fun by Sharon Dlugosch, Florence Nelson

Games for Baby Shower Fun by Sharon Dlugosch

Baby Shower Fun by Sharon Dlugosch

Kid-Tastic Birthday Parties: The Complete Party Planner for Today's Kids by Jane Chase

Romantic At-Home Dinners: Sneaky Strategies for Couples with Kids by Nan Booth/Gary Fischler

Reunions for Fun-Loving Families by Nancy Funke Bagley

An Anniversary to Remember: Years One to Seventy-five by Cynthia Lueck Sowden

Folding Table Napkins: A New Look at a Traditional Craft by Sharon Dlugosch

Table Setting Guide by Sharon Dlugosch

Tabletop Vignettes by Sharon Dlugosch

Don't Slurp Your Soup: A Basic Guide to Business Etiquette by Elizabeth Craig

Meeting Room Games: Getting Things Done in Committees by Nan Booth

Hit the Ground Running: Communicate Your Way to Success by Cynthia Kreuger

These books are available in selected stores and catalogs. If you're having trouble finding them in your area, send a self-addressed, stamped, business-size envelope and request ordering information from:

Brighton Publications, Inc.
P.O. Box 120706
St. Paul, MN 55112-0706

or call: 1-800-536-BOOK (2665)